T0271402

Knowledge Management and AI in Society 5.0

Society 5.0 points towards a human-centred approach by the use of modern, advanced technologies and artificial intelligence. This book explores and offers an overview of knowledge management embraced in the current scenario of Society 5.0, shedding light on its importance in a society that is increasingly digital and interconnected.

The book enhances current managerial and economic research by offering the 'human' side of knowledge management (KM) intertwined with the use of artificial intelligences (AIs). Each chapter explores KM from a different perspective, including entrepreneurship, innovation, marketing, and strategy, in a theoretical and practical way. They include insights from both practitioners and scholars, enriched by practical tools that can be used during laboratories, workshops, and tutorials. The book presents evidence on how to manage KM and develop new knowledge in different subjects, with the aim of overcoming conventional KM strategy and showing how business and society are connected with 'power of subjective human knowledge creation'.

Offering new insights, research and practical guidance, this book will appeal to academics and students of knowledge management as well as digital transformation practitioners looking for ways to transition their organisations from knowledge economy to digital economy.

Manlio Del Giudice is Full Professor of Management at the University of Rome 'Link Campus'. He holds a PhD in Management from the University of Milano-Bicocca and he built his academic and scientific career outside of Italy for more than 12 years, in a wide number of world-renowned universities, prior to coming back to Italy on 2014. He had been hired as full professor in 2018 as one of the 20 youngest professors in Italy, in every scientific field. For more than four years, he has served as editor-in-chief of the top-tier *Journal of Knowledge Management* (WoS Impact Factor 2020: 8.182, ranked #3 in the world in Information Science and Library Science and #9 in Management), and he holds key editorial positions with several international mainstream scientific journals on management (for example, *Journal of Business Research, Journal of International Management, International Entrepreneurship and Management Journal, IEEE Transactions on Engineering Management, Technological Forecasting and Social Change* etc.). His research studies comprise more than 160 publications and have been internationally recognised as having a significant impact, as evidenced by the approximately12,595 citations and the H-index = 55 he has received (as of October 2022) and by his more than 60 publications in only ABS 3* and 4* journals in the last three years. He has served as keynote speaker at top global conferences on management (about 50 per year). Recently, it has been indicated among the most influential scientific profiles in research worldwide according to the data for updated science-wide author databases of standardised citation indicators 2019 developed by the Stanford University, ranking first among Italian full professors in the field of managerial research and in twenty-first place in the homologous category, worldwide (August 2022). He served in several governance apical roles in Italian universities: he has served as associate dean in the Faculty of Economics at the Link Campus University in Rome and, in the same university, he was deputy chancellor, overseeing administration of the Naples campus for more than three years. At the Link Campus Rome, he serves as deputy chancellor for the Erasmus Programme, as well as holding the positions of director of the CERMES Research Centre, director of the Postgraduate Master's in Smart Public Administration and Coordinator of the PhD programme 'Tech for Good'. He acted as international evaluator or consultant for several institutions at national and international level for applied research funded projects. His main research interests deal with knowledge management, technology transfer, foresight management, innovation and technology management.

Veronica Scuotto (PhD, FHEA, MBA, BA-Honour) is currently an Associate Professor in the Department of Economics, Management, Institutions at the University of Naples Federico II (Italy) after working at the University of Turin, at the University of the West of Scotland (UK), and at the Pôle Universitaire Léonard de Vinci in Paris (France). She obtained the Italian National Qualification as full professor in 2020. She has been invited as a guest speaker to several conferences. Her research is focused on small to medium enterprises, knowledge management and digital technologies, which has resulted in the publication of articles featured in top-tier peer-reviewed journals. She has authored three books. Veronica is editorial assistant for the *Journal of Intellectual Capital* and an editorial board member of the *Journal of Knowledge Management*. Veronica is also a member of the International Council for Small Business and is a mentor for the Techstars Smart Mobility Accelerator in Turin, Italy.

Armando Papa, PhD, is currently Associate Professor of Management at the Faculty of Communication Sciences, University of Teramo. He earned the Italian National Qualification as full professor in 2020. Earlier, he joined the University of Rome Universitas Mercatorum. He was formerly a research fellow at ICxT Innovation Center, University of Turin. He holds a PhD in Management from the University of Naples Federico II and a Postgraduate Master in Finance (2011). He is also member of the EuroMed Research Business Institute. He won the Best Paper Award at the Ninth EuroMed Conference in Warsaw (Poland) in 2016. He is skilled in knowledge management, open innovation and technology entrepreneurship, corporate governance and family business. He is associate editor of the *Journal of Knowledge Economy* (Springer) and managing editor of the *Journal of Knowledge Management* (Emerald). He is listed as innovation manager at the Italian Ministry of Economic Development. He has engaged in various peer-review processes for several ranked and outstanding international management journals. He is an editorial board member for the *Journal of Intellectual Capital, British Food Journal, Management Research Review,* and other international journals. He is member of the I.P.E. Business School of Naples.

Routledge Focus on Business and Management

The fields of business and management have grown exponentially as areas of research and education. This growth presents challenges for readers trying to keep up with the latest important insights. *Routledge Focus on Business and Management* presents small books on big topics and how they intersect with the world of business research.

Individually, each title in the series provides coverage of a key academic topic, whilst collectively, the series forms a comprehensive collection across the business disciplines.

Systems Thinking and Sustainable Healthcare Delivery
Ben Fong

Gender Diversity and Inclusion at Work
Divergent Views from Turkey
Zeynep Özsoy, Mustafa Şenyücel and Beyza Oba

Management and Visualisation
Seeing Beyond the Strategic
Gordon Fletcher

Knowledge Management and AI in Society 5.0
Manlio Del Giudice, Veronica Scuotto and Armando Papa

The Logistics Audit
Methods, Organization and Practice
Piotr Buła and Bartosz Niedzielski

For more information about this series, please visit: www.routledge.com/Routledge-Focus-on-Business-and-Management/book-series/FBM

Knowledge Management and AI in Society 5.0

Manlio Del Giudice, Veronica Scuotto, and Armando Papa

Routledge
Taylor & Francis Group

LONDON AND NEW YORK

First published 2023
by Routledge
4 Park Square, Milton Park, Abingdon, Oxon OX14 4RN

and by Routledge
605 Third Avenue, New York, NY 10158

Routledge is an imprint of the Taylor & Francis Group, an informa business

British Library Cataloguing-in-Publication Data
A catalogue record for this book is available from the British Library

ISBN: 978-1-032-19191-1 (hbk)
ISBN: 978-1-032-19192-8 (pbk)
ISBN: 978-1-003-25805-6 (ebk)

DOI: 10.4324/9781003258056

Typeset in Times New Roman
by Newgen Publishing UK

Contents

Introduction

This book analyses how the disruptive power of digitisation is becoming a major challenge for knowledge-based value creation worldwide by emphasising a meso and micro level perspective across organisations. It points up the business and government orientation towards a human-centred approach by the use of the modern and advanced technologies that can be categorised in artificial intelligences (AIs). We offer business with a human face where new knowledge (e.g. innovation) is created by human capital.

Our book advances the body of knowledge from 4.0 to 5.0 by highlighting at the micro and meso level how the interaction dynamics of knowledge management (KM) and AIs impacts positively on the decision-making for particular processes.

By researching and teaching KM for more than 20 years, the authors want to provide an advanced overview of KM exploring the scenario of Society 5.0. It enhances the current managerial and economic research by offering the 'human' side of KM intertwined with the use of AIs. Each chapter argues KM mainly focuses on AIs across four domains such as creativity, innovation, marketing, and strategy. Those domains are analysed mixing a theoretical and practical approach. For instance, starting from the specific literature of a domain, each chapter is finalised with a workshop description along with a special section of 'insights of an expert'. The workshop assumes the form of an experiential laboratory where each participant uses the theoretical sections of the book in a real-life situation.

Overall, the book presents clues on how to manage KM and develop new knowledge in different subjects (e.g. creativity, innovation, marketing, and strategy). The scope is to overcome the conventional KM strategy and show how business and society are connected with 'power of subjective human knowledge creation'. Yet, to overcome the common fear that AIs may completely replace humans, the book casts

DOI: 10.4324/9781003258056-1

the light on how the power of human knowledge creation along with AIs and encapsulates the essence of modern Society 5.0. Human KM deals with social and economic problems, shifting the entire society into an entrepreneurial laboratory. The discovery of this book concerns how to bring value into a business and society.

Takeaways

The present book offers a new hyper/word, that is human KM. It thus enhances the current KM literature primarily focused on the evolution of KM in the business world with less attention to the human side.
In this regard, the takeaways of this book can be synthetised as follows:

- Walk the reader through the definition of KM, AIs in the scenario of Society 5.0
- Understand how KM is empowered by AI
- Provide a practical guidance for identifying the best practices to manage knowledge
- Offer practical tools to experience and valorise the human side of KM
- Present new ways to stimulate knowledge workers and citizens in developing new innovative ideas
- Suggest insights from practitioners that can intertwine theory and real world
- Recommend new future research directions
- Propose new hyper-words

Chapter Synopsis

The introduction section, thus, summarises the main concepts of the book, stimulating 'appetite' and more interest in discovering the book. It offers aims and how, why, and who the book should be read.

Chapter 1 entitled 'Knowledge Management and AIs for Creativity' introduces the concept of KM and AIs and their linkage in encouraging creativity within a business as a form of intrapreneurship and outside as a form of entrepreneurship in the context of Society 5.0. In this context, the authors suggest the outlook of the modern, current society where the combination of economic men and citizens generates new knowledge supported by AIs. The current chapter offers a workshop to let participants (e.g. students and/or practitioners) to experience the theory based on KM and AI for creativity. Additionally, the chapter offers a special section where Professor Norris Krueger from

University of Kyushu argues the concept of KM considering its impact on ecosystems, open innovation approach, and AIs.

Chapter 2 entitled 'Knowledge Management and AIs for Innovation' looks inside the innovation perspective provoking everyone to have an entrepreneurial mind. This has resulted in an open innovation approach where everyone (e.g. customers, employees, founders, and so on) will have the function to destroy and create new knowledge to make an impact on the overall society. In turn, innovation is driven by social needs empowered by humans. In this context, AIs embrace the powerful role of harnessing existing and new knowledge. The current chapter offers a workshop to participants (e.g. students and/or practitioners) to experience the theory based on KM and AI per innovation. Furthermore, the chapter provides a special section by Professor Noboru Konno from Tama University, Tokyo, Japan, who discusses the KM process in relation to innovation by the use of AIs.

Chapter 3 entitled 'Knowledge Management and AIs for Marketing' argues the KM on the marketing perspective. It offers a customer/centric approach, introducing a modern view of marketing, namely marketing 5.0. In this context the KM designs users' experience and AIs serve humans to create a multi modal lean and agile IT landscape. The current chapter offers a workshop to participants (e.g. students and/or practitioners) to experience the theory based on KM and AI per marketing. Furthermore, the chapter provides a special section by Professor Khelladi Insaf from Léonard de Vinci Pôle Universitaire, and Professor Castellano Sylvaine from Métis Lab, EM Normandie Business School. They offer a new view of the role of AI in managing and creating knowledge in marketing.

Chapter 4 entitled 'Knowledge Management and AIs for Strategy' debates the KM in the strategy outlook. It involves an orchestration AI platform where the human side of the economy (e.g. economic men, consumers, knowledge workers, and citizens) develops new strategies. It considers how the relationship between KM and AI supports the operations and the functions for business. The current chapter offers a workshop to participants (e.g. students and/or practitioners) to experience the theory based on KM and AI per strategy. Furthermore, the chapter provides a special section by Professor Vijay Pereira from Neoma Business School who discusses the effective allocation of KM in relation to data-driven strategy by in AI context.

In the concluding section, the authors discuss the hyper-word, human KM, and how it is emerged supported by AIs in the current scenario of Society 5.0. In this vein, the book helps KM community to report on progress against goals and targets in terms that are understandable and comparable to their organisational peers, to explain how an organisational culture and management philosophy should be aligned with the upcoming vision of the digital knowledge intensive organisations and contribute to achieving the new vision, and to spread how leaders and entrepreneurs can engage their organisation in evaluation the technology progress and the innovation readiness against the vision of technological and interchangeable human KM model.

Target Audience

The book is useful and recommended as a special section for courses in Entrepreneurship, Strategic Marketing, Fundamentals of Management, Innovation Management and Digital Transformation, Business Creation, Digital Marketing, and Customer Knowledge Management. Therefore, the main audience for this book would include master students in KM and business management programmes. The secondary audience is KM practitioners and academics, primarily individuals who are responsible for digital transformation leaders in any kind of organisation. Practitioners also include consultants and professionals along with business managers who might be looking for ways to transition their organisations from Industry 4.0 to Society 5.0 by adopting a human-centred approach. Authors' intention is to reach the business consulting teams, entrepreneurs, and executive directors (especially for small business) across all sectors interested in new frontiers of human–technology interaction. Hence, the book provides a user-friendly and smart framework to contextualise the emergent topic across the main functions for the business. Yet, we expect to be appealing for different countries such as Italy, France, UK, Germany, Asian, Middle East, and Northern Africa Region, and Australia.

1 Knowledge Management and AIs for Creativity

'If you have one dollar to invest in knowledge management, put one cent into information management and 99 cents into human interaction'.

Prusak L., 2018

The world has changed. Is this due to COVID-19? No, it is not just that. The change started at the beginning of globalisation, leading to digital transformation that has brought new advanced technologies like artificial intelligences (AIs). It has increased the level of complexity but also offered new opportunities. The level of innovation gets higher along with the degree of expectations. New tools are offered to customers to better experience this new virtual reality: for example, Google oculus allows us to explore reality from a completely different perspective by presenting the chance to 'play and live' in a virtual reality. Companies embrace a new approach that sets aside implementation and planning and relies on discovery and exploration, trying to face uncertainty and complexity. Imagine you are standing on a chair that is leaning against a wall. How would you feel? This may describe the state of unbalance and uncertainty that the 'new' world has brought.

Starting from what we know to do can be the right thing, to understand how to get a competitive advantage. Would be this enough? The current economic scenario requires the involvement of an international and domestic ecosystem that forges 'what we know' and steers 'how we do things', which consequently generates awareness around 'why we do things'. The three steps of What, How, and Why generate value that is focused on offering new alternatives compared with the existing ones to customers, employees, business partners, and so on, who wonder what effect a business can have in the innovation process. In turn, companies are not just guided by the economic and financial pillar but by sustainability, which includes ethics, environmental, and social concerns.

DOI: 10.4324/9781003258056-2

Sustainability requires an ecosystem and people, nurturing the development of collective knowledge that is rooted by internal, existing knowledge and external, explicit, knowledge. People are the focus point of the modern economy that has been humanised and converted from Industry 4.0 to Society 5.0 (Fukuyama, 2018; Yabanci, 2020).

The use of AIs allows customers to visualise what there is behind a product production, avoiding asymmetric information and knowledge hiding. Such technologies have also revolutionised the way of making and doing business: it has introduced four AI business patterns: 1) AIs for local business, 2) AIs for interaction, 3) AIs for repositioning, and 4) AIs for sustainability.

AIs for local business means helping the domestic market overcome local boundaries and be able to reach worldwide customers. It is a way of facilitating and replacing human routines; AIs analyse the environment to simulate individual behaviour, although, it is well recognised that AIs cannot fully replace individuals due to the limits on their mental process in terms of creativity and problem-solving. Therefore, the emerging fear of 'job-killing robots' will not occur. AIs will not scrap jobs but empower them. As Stigltz (2018; 2011) stated that such technologies are highly beneficial for individuals because they equip them with new capabilities. Accordingly, Del Giudice et al. (2022) empirically show that robots (also named humanoids) marginally or completely modify routines, which indirectly impacts labour productivity. In doing so, senior leaders are induced to create a balance between explorative and exploitative routines. Explorative routines require creativity and critical thinking, while exploitative routines rely on repetitive and imitative activities. In this sense, we suggest that AIs for local business indicate the relevance of bootlegging creativity and problem-solving. In a nutshell, it encourages entrepreneurship in terms of enterprising actions and an entrepreneurial mindset. In 1990, Morning Star (consulting company) introduced a new managerial approach, removing all managers and giving more responsibilities to all employees. This approach is considered a self-management approach where all employees manage themselves and mediate responsibilities with their colleagues. Nowadays, AIs are elected to enforce such a managerial approach and emphasise the relevance of a human-centred approach.

AIs for interactions derives from the connection of different smart devices that interact like individuals (Kamble & Shah, 2018). In turn, individuals feel alienated in a job task and psychologically stressed (Braganza et al., 2021) even though AIs have brought new benefits such as preserving individual experiences and knowledge; offering specialised solutions; avoiding annoyance; and saving time and costs of individual effort (Alhawamdeh et al., 2020). Such technologies have provoked a 'lateral exchange of ideas', considering that territorial and cognitive boundaries are removed. Knowledge circulates freely and so companies can take new ideas from 'the wisdom of crowds' (Surowiecki, 2005), that is, non-experts who are able to bring up new ideas more than experts. Companies can exploit consumer data received through the interaction with them and improve 'customer-centric insights', which is valuable for idea generation (Newman, 2019). For example, the current era is overwhelmed by recommendations or reviews about a destination, restaurant, shop and so on (Bi et al., 2019). Such recommendations are mostly used to improve existing products or to discover new needs and generate a new product/service.

AIs for repositioning refers to the change that embracing companies, markets, the environment and individuals are embracing. It is necessary to offer new directions that express the change in knowledge and in the managerial approach. AIs cause a cobotisation effect (Battaglia, 2021), which repositions the role of technologies within a company, setting a level of efficacy and efficiency that helps employees reach their goals. Accordingly, repositioning towards new frontiers protects individual knowledge and presents new renewal opportunities. Such frontiers can be recognised in the form of intrapreneurship, which encourages a new entrepreneurial spirit within an organisational setting. The historic business founded by Enrico Loccioni in Ancona represents this vision of uplifting the entrepreneurial behaviour of employees and acquiring new knowledge and skills.

AI for sustainability is based on the fact that customers need to trust 'you'. The relevance of achieving the United Nation Sustainable Development Goals (SDGs) is evident in any kind of social, political and economic domain. AIs are playing a relevant role in reducing carbon emissions, in converting cities into smart cities, in resource conservation and so on (Nishant et al., 2020). AIs are considered tools for employing design thinking and innovation models focusing on 'design for environment and eco-design' (McDonough & Braungart, 2010). This involves close collaboration between researchers and practitioners who come up with new ideas to address real and practical challanges. Through AIs, researchers have access to data and expertise, while practitioners gain new knowledge. IBM Tririga is a system of facility management that employs AIs to optimise energy use in a working space, reducing energy cost and offering a great workplace experience for employees.

Therefore, AIs are revolutionising the way of making and running a business, and what about managing knowledge? It has been observed that AIs are focused on knowledge (Jakubczyc & Owoc, 1998). In the current human-centred orientation, knowledge needs AIs and vice versa to improve business performance. The process of knowledge management (KM) is based on acquiring new knowledge, adopting existing knowledge, combining new and existing knowledge and integrating them within a company. Preserving such knowledge and updating knowledge or changing to a knowledge creation process is supported by AIs. AIs comprehend a 'knowledge-based system life cycle' and a KM system (Scuotto & Mueller, 2018). Accordingly, KM moves in two directions: one is based on constructing AIs and the other one is management individual and collective knowledge (Sveiby, 1998).

KM, AIs, and Creativity

As outlined, AIs are a relevant tool in the process of knowledge creation. Knowledge creation is stimulated by technology-driven innovations like AIs. AIs are currently supporting entrepreneurs and intrapreneurs (in the next chapter, we use the concept of innovator) in sharing and developing new ideas along with making new collaborations. We consider the definition of AIs as a 'computer-controlled robot' that carries out smart tasks to improve business learnings and problem-solving tasks (Copeland, 2020). Basically, AIs optimise employees' jobs and sustain work–life equilibrium (Milenkovic, 2019). Considering creativity, AIs have been used to make a new painting, like a new robot artist (Haynes, 2019), or to assist in cooking activities (Whyte, 2019). AIs free up individual working time and offer new opportunities to generate innovations through the enormous amount of data that they can provide. In this sense, knowledge would not produce exciting ideas if it were not supported by AIs. It is a combination of human and machine to trigger individual creativity (Shneiderman, 2020). For instance, the company Brandmark.io is a 'smart logo-generating tool' through AIs that support the creative process of logo creation (Hisrich & Soltanifar, 2021). Nevertheless, the creativity aspect still relies on human behaviour and judgement and goes beyond AI features. In turn, AIs can systematically collect all ideas and stimulate individual thinking outside the box. AIs can be considered a method to make innovations. In this sense, this scenario represents the shift from Industry 4.0 (mostly focused on technologies) to Society 5.0 (primarily based on humans). Therefore, reflecting upon the intertwining among KM, AIs, and creativity, and how and why it would be beneficial for a company, we took into consideration Wolcott and Lippitz's (2007; see also Battaglia, 2021) model on corporate entrepreneurship. In this specific case, we replace corporate entrepreneurship with intrapreneurship because it gives more the sense of individual knowledge and creation. These authors have identified four archetypes of intrapreneurship: 1) Enabler, 2) Producer, 3) Opportunist, and 4) Advocate that stem from the connection between resource authority (ad hoc and dedicated) and organisational ownership (diffused and focused). In another approach, we have maintained the same archetypes but associated with two other variables: AI technology adoption (ad hoc for a specific business unit or dedicated to a certain project); and KM process (collective and individual) (Figure 1.1).

Although all four archetypes derive from the combination of KM process and AI adoption, the different levels of such combination offer a different model. For instance, the enabler model is formed by the high collective KM process and a dedicated AI adoption. This model involves a collective knowledge entity, which means that a group of people undertake the same tasks and reach a common goal. Accordingly, AI adoption is aimed at a specific project, but it may disappear when the project is concluded. Yet, people are inclined to adopt AIs as it is part of the organisational culture, and creativity is enabled and empowered by the collective knowledge.

The opportunist model concerns a collective KM process and so a collective entity of knowledge that comes from a team working on a

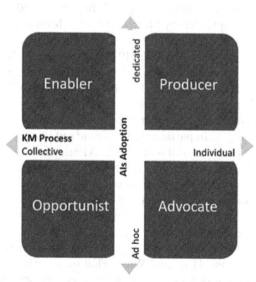

Figure 1.1 Four archetypes of intrapreneurship.
Source: Authors' elaboration.

project of a specific business unit that adopts AIs. It is limited to a certain department and does not allow for a cross-functional approach. Creativity can emerge through a few people and they can scatter because the organisational environment is not inclined towards new ideas.

The advocate model shows ad hoc AI adoption associated with individual KM processes. The spread of knowledge and consequently of creativity comes from a single person. In turn, tacit knowledge becomes relevant in this model, where an individual spreads creativity belonging to a distinct business unit that adopts AIs. Such individuals can assume the role of 'evangelist of innovation'.

The producer model is composed of individual KM processes and dedicated AI adoption. Accordingly, when AI adoption is dedicated to a certain project, it involves the organisational setting and so it is part of the organisational culture. Creativity is generated by a single person who can produce innovation as a new company (namely industry spinoff). In turn, from being an intrapreneur, that individual becomes an entrepreneur who exploits opportunities (from both an internal organisational setting and external one) to generate new innovations.

The intertwining of the KM process and AI adoption are linked to individual and team creativity, that is, the ability to exploit internal opportunities to introduce a new solution to a problem. According to de Carvalho Botega and da Silva (2020), creativity is a solution to a problem that involves an ecosystem (this aspect is fully explained in the special section of this chapter led by Norris Krueger). Moreover, it is also relevant to mention the emotional side of being a creative intrapreneur or entrepreneur. Since Amabile (1997), the sense of loving one's job has been considered crucial to enhance the intrinsic motivation to think outside the box. Recently, Scuotto and Farronato (2021) have deeply explored the concept of love in a start-up journey. They have investigated different case studies and some of them were placed in the context of Society 5.0. In particular, they found out that love and entrepreneurship can coexist as well as love and AI adoption so as to generate new innovations. Based on this emotional pattern of an entrepreneur, we maintain the need for openness to change and unlock the talent in a single person (Kegan & Lahey, 2009). Accordingly, we propose a new workshop idea that can stimulate participants (e.g. students and/or practitioners) to experience their creativity and their learning. The workshop encourages to develop a new creative solution based on the three pillars of What, How, and Why: What means what is the problem to solve; How considers how the problem can be solved by adopting AIs; and Why concerns the value that can be generated for an entire society, for a company and for each individual.

Workshop: What, How, and Why in Five Steps

The present workshop aims to reflect upon the current market situation and individuate a problem. The scope is to come up with a solution that involves the use of AIs. The participants do not need to use the AIs as they usually do but should create a new way of using such technologies in their solution. Moreover, it provokes the 'use' of individual and collective knowledge. Additionally, through the workshop participants are able to reflect upon their own skills and work in a team.

The workshop requires creativity and imagination that can be transformed into a real business (how to do that will be explained in the next chapter).

We have identified five steps: 1) Individuating the problem; 2) Team development and picking a single problem as a collective choice; 3) Coming up with a new solution; 4) Describing how to adopt AIs; 5) Pitching a solution. The mentor/lecturer steers the four stages, setting the time and checking team commitment and engagement.

1. Individuating the problem: each participant defines a problem that can concern professional or personal or community life. Such a problem is described in the form of a brief in order to explain what are the challenges and the opportunities that can emerge. In this first stage, the participant reflects upon the current situation individually in order to 'nurture' the tacit, internal knowledge (time is set for up to ten minutes);
2. Team development and picking a single problem as a collective choice: the mentor/lecturer invites the participants to form a group of five people maximum. Each participant presents their own identity card defining qualities in terms of being *an innovator, a rationalist; an evaluator; a controller; a resource hunting; a trader and a technical specialist* (time is set for up to 15 minutes). Then, each participant shows the brief in order to pick the single problem to work on. There is not bad or good idea/choice; this is just a collective choice (time is set for up 25 to minutes);
3. Coming up with a new solution; this stage can be also named an experiential laboratory where each participant will 'experience' the process of coming up with a solution. In turn, it requires a shift from individual knowledge and skill to collective ones. The group interacts and discusses their own ideas. They should think about their own ecosystem in order to figure out the resources (in terms of capital; technology; infrastructure and so on) to develop their idea. It is important that the group assume a self-management approach. They start to draft their solution, describing qualities, opportunities and potential challenges (time is set for up to 25 minutes);
4. Describing how to adopt AIs within a business; this stage requires thinking about the four AIs business patterns: 1) AIs for local business; 2) AIs for interaction; 3) AIs for repositioning; and 4) AIs for sustainability. In doing so, each group individuates a suitable pattern for the solution and explains how those technologies can be used and the opportunities that can emerge (time is set for up to 25 minutes);
5. Pitching a solution; this is the last stage where each group starts to think of how to make a pitch. Each group should think about how to sell the solution and why, in terms of the value that it can generate for the business and for the entire ecosystem. In particular, the group will present:
   – What is the problem?

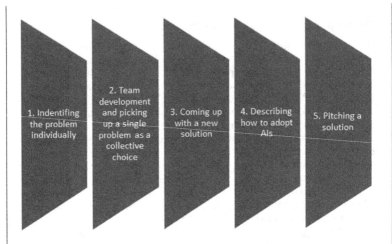

Figure 1.2 What, How, and Why I in five steps.
Source: Authors' elaboration.

– How is the problem solved (in terms of solution and AI adoption)?
– Why can that solution generate value for the business and the ecosystem?
  Going back to step 2; each participant will integrate 'own quality' into the pitch. Therefore, to sum up: each participant introduces him/herself, specifying their own 'quality' and then 'selling the idea' in a time frame of ten minutes.

  Each pitch presents its own idea in front of potential investors like the *Shark Tank* live television show. It should be a real-life investment pitch. Good luck! (Figure 1.2).

  In concluding, the mentor/lecturer invites all students to reflect upon their activities and give five types of reflections: what happened? (narrate); what did they feel? (emotional); what are their thoughts about the workshop? (perception); what were the new parts taken during those stages? (analytical); what was good or bad? (evaluative); and what would they have done differently? (critical) (Neck et al., 2014).

References

Alhawamdeh, A. K., Alghizzawi, M., & Habes, M. (2020). The relationship between media marketing advertising and encouraging Jordanian women to conduct early detection of breast cancer. *European Journal of Business and Management, 12*(2020), 130–135.

Amabile, T. M. (1997). Motivating creativity in organizations: On doing what you love and loving what you do. *California Management Review, 40*(1), 39–58.

Battaglia, R. (2021). *Company startuppers: Unlocking the hidden entrepreneurial potential in our organizations.* Milan: EGEA.

Bi, J. W., Liu, Y., Fan, Z. P., & Zhang, J. (2019). Wisdom of crowds: Conducting importance-performance analysis (IPA) through online reviews. *Tourism Management, 70,* 460–478.

Braganza, A., Chen, W., Canhoto, A., & Sap, S. (2021). Productive employment and decent work: The impact of AI adoption on psychological contracts, job engagement and employee trust. *Journal of Business Research, 131,* 485–494.

Copeland, B. J. (2020). Artificial intelligence. Retrieved on 9 September 2021 from www.britannica.com/technology/artificialintelligence/Reasoning.

de Carvalho Botega, L. F., & da Silva, J. C. (2020). An artificial intelligence approach to support knowledge management on the selection of creativity and innovation techniques. *Journal of Knowledge Management, 24*(5), 1107–1130. https://doi.org/10.1108/JKM-10-2019-0559

Del Giudice, M., Scuotto, V., Ballestra, L. V., & Pironti, M. (2022). Humanoid robot adoption and labour productivity: a perspective on ambidextrous product innovation routines. *The International Journal of Human Resource Management, 33*(6), 1098–1124.

Del Giudice, M., Scuotto, V., Orlando, B., & Mustilli, M. (2023). Toward the human-centered approach: A revised model of individual acceptance of AI. *Human Resource Management Review, 33*(1), 100856.

Fukuyama, M. (2018). Society 5.0: Aiming for a new human-centered society. *Japan Spotlight, 27*(5), 47–50.

Haynes, S. (2019, 17 June). This robot artist just became the first to stage a solo exhibition. What does that say about creativity? *Time* magazine. https://time.com/5607191/robot-artist-ai-da-artificial-intelligence-creativity/

Hisrich, R. D., & Soltanifar, M. (2021). Unleashing the creativity of entrepreneurs with digital technologies. In Mariusz Soltanifar, Mathew Hughes, and Lutz Göcke (Eds.), *Digital Entrepreneurship* (pp. 23–49). Cham: Springer.

Jakubczyc, J. A., & Owoc, M. L. (1998). Knowledge management and artificial intelligence. *Argumenta Oeconomica, 1*(6).

Kamble, R., & Shah, D. (2018). Applications of artificial intelligence in human life. *International journal of research-Granthaalayah, 6*(6), 178–188.

Kegan, R., & Lahey, L. L. (2009). *Immunity to change: How to overcome it and unlock potential in yourself and your organization.* Boston: Harvard Business Press.

Milenkovic, J. (2019). Astounding artificial intelligence statistics for 2020. Retrieved on 21 September 2021 from https://kommandotech. com/statistics/artificial-intelligence-statistics/

Neck, H. M., Greene, P. G., & Brush, C. G. (Eds.). (2014). *Teaching entrepreneurship: A practice-based approach.* Cheltenham, UK: Edward Elgar.

Newman, D. (2019, 16 April). 5 ways AI is transforming the customer experience. *Forbes*. www. forbes.com/sites/danielnewman/2019/04/16/5-ways-ai-is-transforming-the-customer-experience/#72b43c53465a

Nishant, R., Kennedy, M., & Corbett, J. (2020). Artificial intelligence for sustainability: Challenges, opportunities, and a research agenda. *International Journal of Information Management, 53*, 102104.

Scuotto, V., & Mueller, J. (2018). *ICT adoption for knowledge management: Opportunities for SMEs*. Oxford: RossiSmith.

Surowiecki, J. (2005). *The wisdom of crowds*. New York: Anchor.

Sveiby, K. E. (1998). Measuring intangibles and intellectual capital-an emerging first standard. *Communications and Network, 9*(1).

Whyte, C. (2019, 10 January). AI created images of food just by reading the recipes. New Scientist. www.newscientist. com/article/2190259-ai-created-images-of-food-just-by-reading-the-recipes/#ixzz6K6GK35So.

Wolcott, R. C., & Lippitz, M. J. (2007, 1 October). The four models of corporate entrepreneurship. *MIT Sloan Management Review, 49*(1), 75.

SPECIAL SECTION

Norris Krueger[1]

The Real 'New Normal'?

Why are so many people not seeing just how much innovation has changed in the last decade? We love to talk about the 'new normal' because of COVID-19, but we need to realise that much of that 'new' normal was already there! However, the real epiphany for me came back in 2010.[2] As we will see, we have only scratched the surface of potential research opportunities.

Consider how we are talking so much about the massive dislocations globally in supply chains. Yes, COVID-19 has wreaked havoc on supply chains, but the real message is that supply chains were already damaged for years as we arrogantly 'optimised' supply chains to squeeze out any redundancy (e.g. Sanders, 2020). Of course, it is easy to see today that we squeezed out most of the resilience. It is not as easy to see that this also squeezed all the opportunities to learn from a richer, more diverse set of existing and potential suppliers. Cue Ashby's Law of Requisite Variety?

To paraphrase the old maxim, 'Adversity does not forge character, adversity reveals it', COVID has revealed so much that was already normal and laid bare how an extended economic expansion had encouraged a 'normal' that turned out to be unsustainable.

It's a Rainforest World

We also may pay considerable lip service to the notion that Industry 4.0 compels us to think in terms of ecosystems (e.g. Müller et al., 2018; Rüßmann et al., 2015). Great! But why do we try to optimise ecosystems? To borrow one of my favourite metaphors, this is like trying to optimise a rainforest like we try to optimise a farm. Even though it, unsurprisingly, does not work for entrepreneurship and innovation, nonetheless we definitely still try to optimise innovation ecosystems. Worse, we too often find misleading evidence when we optimise during boom times (Brett, 2019; Hwang & Horowitt, 2012).

The recurring problem is that ecosystems are driven more bottom-up by their various participants than by the power players. Ecosystems offer a complex, dynamic (and adaptive) web of stakeholders; only rarely are nice tidy linear relationships in play. However, scholars and practitioners alike keep looking for the linearities. While research from this perspective is growing, more work is definitely needed and would be most welcomed by practitioners and policymakers.[3]

From a knowledge management perspective, we lose most of the information and knowledge that we might have gained from our organisation being embedded in a more complex, diverse community. Ask yourself this: If we were looking for new molecules/compounds to advance medical care, would you look in a farm or in a rainforest?

Open Innovation: Best Way to Navigate a Rainforest?

Back in 2010, at an International Council for Small Businesses[4] conference in Cincinnati, I met Christopher Theon, head of knowledge management[5] at consumer product giant Procter & Gamble. He shared P&G's exciting open innovation (OI) initiative, Connect and Develop.[6] Seeing how P&G had built a robust community where knowledge spillover was truly multilateral, was a game changer. Leveraging co-opetition was so logical.

If P&G cannot turn intellectual property (IP) into a billion-dollar product, it is too small for P&G to commit strategic resources towards. So why not try to find it a 'good home'? Handing it to the right small/medium-sized firm, maybe even a start-up (or spinout) benefits customers and builds the community even more. For another example, if P&G is stuck on, for example, a packaging problem, why not ask the community? Then hire two or three to solve it for you?

This OI model was somewhat rare back then, but has become more widespread than I could have dreamed.[7] Since then, it has exploded globally (e.g. Orlando et al., 2020; Scuotto et al., 2020; West & Bogers, 2014). Google 'Grand Challenges' and it is not just governments, think tanks, and non-government organizations (NGOs). Many corporate behemoths have stepped up and found new competitive advantages as OI is also a powerful tool for organisations which are good at execution to leverage those capabilities.

It's Not the Idea, It's the Execution

We hear that all the time, but OI lives by that assumption. Once you can execute an idea better than anyone else, should it really matter who owns the IP?

Of course, this multilateral spillover that may also be in constant flux will challenge organisations still committed to the traditional strategy of controlling IP closely and licensing judiciously. We need more research into how firms have successfully (and unsuccessfully) navigated that process.

Channelling Van Gogh? (Ambidexterity Meets Co-opetition)

On the other hand, OI also offers significant value for experts at opportunity exploitation to rapidly gain expertise at opportunity exploration. A firm's 'R & D department' includes the exploration of its partners. One does not have to be a manufacturer to understand that being ambidextrous – skilled at both exploitation and exploration (Guerrero, 2021) – energises sustainable competitive advantage. We can look at artists (who borrow from each other routinely). Fascinating recent studies on Vincent Van Gogh found that his work took off when he began to master both exploration and exploitation via new ideas and more skilled techniques (Liu et al., 2021). In the entrepreneurial world, we are familiar with corporate spin-outs where IP and talent exit the larger organisation. More recently, Michl et al. (2012) noted the rise of the 'spin-along', where the spinout is encouraged, supported and monitored by the parent organisation in a coopetition model. Again, ambidexterity offers important phenomena to study.

What Does This Mean for Knowledge Management?

While OI has strong roots in knowledge management, it and Industry 4.0 in general have profound implications for knowledge management. If much of the relevant, actionable knowledge to manage is external and accruing from disparate sources, then what should we expect to be growing in importance? What phenomena should be most profitable for research studies?

Learning ecosystems: If industry is an ecosystem or set of ecosystems, creating a learning ecosystem is imperative. We have observed that a healthy entrepreneurial ecosystem is mutually reinforced by an entrepreneurship education ecosystem (e.g. OECD/EU 2018; ICSB, 2021). If we are to maximise the impacts of multilateral spillover, organisations need to develop a productive learning ecosystem. What are effective organisations doing to promote this? What are the unsuccessful ones doing?

Learning mindset: At the same time, we are beginning to understand the vital importance of a learning mindset that encourages learning and nudges it in productive directions. Again, what are effective organisations doing? What are the unsuccessful doing?

What Does This Mean for Strategy?

We read today often about 'stakeholder capitalism', but as we might guess from the foregoing, smart organisations have always preferred a multilateral strategy where they negotiated with various stakeholders, often in non-linear fashion (Mitchell et al., 1997). Still, gone are the days where we might routinely analyse dyadic relationships such as firm–customer, firm–supplier, firm– employee or firm–investor.

Blurred Lines?[8]

Whether we call it OI or coopetition, this blurs the lines between customer, supplier, and competitor. Industry 4.0 is called the 'Connected Age'[9] for good reason. In product market A, you might be my best supplier; in product market B, I might be your best supplier; and in product market C, we compete ferociously. Today, this is not remotely odd. And today it has become a source of sustainable competitive advantage.

Notes

1 PhD; Visiting Research Professor, QREC at the University of Kyushu, Fukuoka, Japan; Visiting Professor, University of Management & Technology, Lahore, Pakistan; norris.krueger@gmail.com
2 Stay tuned – more on that later.
3 Productive, well-attended workshops and symposia at recent conferences of the Academy of Management and ICSB.

4 International Council for Small Business, www.icsb.org
5 Interestingly, Theon was also apparently Director of Innovation for P&G, a unique (and accidental) confluence of roles that was the difference-maker.
6 www.pgconnectdevelop.com/
7 In this short space, it is impossible to cover Open Innovation in the detail it deserves. I recommend the interested reader to read the seminal work of Henry Chesbrough and more recent work by Bogers, Orlando, Scuotto, West and others in the bibliography.
8 Interestingly and ironically, the famed song turned out to be itself plagiarised, which is fairly difficult to do as the music industry borrows from each other so often   (www.reuters.com/article/us-music-blurredlines/marvin-gaye-family-prevails-in-blurred-lines-plagiarism-case-idUSKBN1GX27P)
9 'Connected Age' is attributed to marketing guru and author Seth Godin.

References

Brett, A. (2019) *Admired disorder*. New York: BabyBooks.

Guerrero, M. (2021). Ambidexterity and entrepreneurship studies: A literature review and research agenda. *Foundations & Trends® in Entrepreneurship, 17*(5–6), 436–650.

Hwang, V. W., & Horowitt, G. (2012). *The rainforest: The secret to building the next Silicon Valley*. Los Altos Hills, CA: Wiley.

Liu, L., Dehmamy, N., Chown, J., Giles, C. L., & Wang, D. (2021). Understanding the onset of hot streaks across artistic, cultural, and scientific careers. arXiv preprint arXiv:2103.01256.

McDonough, W., & Braungart, M. (2010). *Cradle to cradle: Remaking the way we make things*. New York: North Point Press.

Michl, T., Gold, B., & Picot, A. (2012). The spin-along approach: Ambidextrous corporate venturing management. *International Journal of Entrepreneurship & Small Business, 15*(1), 39–56.

Mitchell, R. K., Agle, B. R., & Wood, D. J. (1997). Toward a theory of stakeholder identification and salience: Defining the principle of who and what really counts. *Academy of Management Review, 22*(4), 853–886.

Müller, J. M., Buliga, O., & Voigt, K.-I. (2018). Fortune favors the prepared: How SMEs approach business model innovations in Industry 4.0. *Technological Forecasting & Social Change, 132*, 2–17.

Orlando, B., Ballestra, L. V., Magni, D., & Ciampi, F. (2020). Open innovation and patenting activity in health care. *Journal of Intellectual Capital, 22*(2), 384–402.

Rüßmann, M., Lorenz, M., Gerbert, P., Waldner, M., Engel, P., Harnisch, M., & Justus, J. (2015, 9 April). Industry 4.0: The future of productivity and growth in manufacturing industries. *Boston Consulting Group*, 54–89.

Sanders, N. R. (2020). *Supply chain management: A global perspective*. Danvers, MA: Wiley Global Education.

Scuotto, V., & Farronato, N. (2021). *Love in start-up era*. Oxford, UK: Rossi Smith Academic Publishing.

Scuotto, V., Beatrice, O., Valentina, C., Nicotra, M., Di Gioia, L., & Briamonte, M. F. (2020). Uncovering the micro-foundations of knowledge sharing in open innovation partnerships: An intention-based perspective of technology transfer. *Technological Forecasting and Social Change, 152*, 119906.

West, J., & Bogers, M. (2014). Leveraging external sources of innovation: A review of research on open innovation. *Journal of Product Innovation Management, 31*(4), 814–831.

2 Knowledge Management and AIs for Innovation

'The only thing that gives an organization a competitive edge, the only thing that is sustainable, is what it knows, how it uses what it knows and how fast it can know something new!'

Prusak L., 1996

Every day, each individual shares knowledge with others, either working for a business or simply having a conversation with another person. With the current human-centred approach, knowledge has assumed a key role in a business environment. It is not just considered a mere intangible asset or resource which refers to the process of understanding (McQueen, 1998) or a state of mind or a combination of values, routines, cultures and so on (Davenport & Prusak, 1998; Churchman, 1971), but knowledge is also a form of individual capabilities (Hamel & Prahalad, 1990) along with skills and information (Stewart, 1997; Agrifoglio, 2015; Alavi & Leidner, 2001) that can also be a collective entity (Nonaka, 1994; Scuotto et al., 2017). Both individual and collective knowledge need to be managed to create something with value. In this sense, the concept of knowledge management (KM) has been embraced in the management system of an enterprise. KM is a process that involves knowledge sharing, integration, absorption, storing and creation (Scuotto & Mueller, 2018; McAdam & Reid, 2001). KM is able to bring out more value from resources that are converted into capabilities (Darroch, 2005). Such value and capabilities can be exploited to generate innovations. Starting from a mere idea, it becomes more structured knowledge and then is turned into invention that can be transformed into a product or service to be commercialised in order to talk about innovation.

By looking back at previous studies, it is possible to highlight the need for innovation in a clearer way. In the past, resources were

DOI: 10.4324/9781003258056-3

primarily recognised as homogeneous and well allocated to generate a market equilibrium and so to make decisions (the main principle of neoclassical microeconomic theory; Penrose, 1959). In turn, this process considers internal resources but it does not take into consideration external resources. This has encouraged the development of the theory of growth for a firm, which inspired the framework of the resource-based view (RBV) (Penrose, 1959) that considers uncertainty and asymmetric information (Coase, 1937; Usai et al., 2018) along with entrepreneurial resourcefulness (Zahra, 2021). The resources are identified as tangible and intangible assets. The tangible assets are identified as infrastructure, machines, financial resources and so on; whereas, the intangible assets are grouped into intellectual capital, which is formed out of human capital, structural capital and relational capital (Dabić et al., 2020). Rather than exploring each resource, it is interesting to consider the value of a resource for its combination with others (Penrose, 1959). The KM combines such resources – mostly intangible resources – and transforms them into capabilities (Nelson & Winter, 1982) or more specific dynamic capabilities (Teece, 2018). Those capabilities concern the ability to solve a problem, to exploit new modes to deal with market changes, and to find a new way of offering a solution (Zahra et al., 2006) and also 'product development, strategic decision making, and alliancing' (Eisenhard & Martin, 2000). In a nutshell, dynamic capabilities can refer to an organisation or a single individual, and in both cases the scope is to generate innovations (Scuotto et al., 2022; 2021) and also make decisions at the right time (Barreto, 2010). Generally speaking, KM supports the development of new capabilities which are crucial for innovations. Evaluating the effectiveness of KM is difficult because it is substantially based on tacit knowledge (Nonaka & Takeuchi, 1995). However, if we consider innovations like products and/or services as KM outputs, it is interesting to explore the dynamic relationship between KM and innovation in the current real world. In the past, scholars have presented some empirical studies showing KM outputs in the form of achieving competitive advantage (Conner & Prahalad, 1996; Guerrero et al., 2019), maintaining intellectual capital (Wiig, 1997; Amjal et al., 2010; Durst & Edvardsson, 2012); and supporting innovations (Du Plessis, 2007; Darrock, 2005; Andreeva & Kianto, 2011; Shujahat et al., 2019) along with competitiveness (Carniero, 2000).

The Concept of Innovation

Before discussing the linkage between KM and innovation in the digital transformation era, a historical excursus of the innovation concept is useful for understanding the changes that have occurred in the current market situation. Innovation is a concept that does not stand alone but is accompanied by creativity and invention. By looking into the process to achieve an innovation, creativity leverages new business ideas and so generates new knowledge to be converted into an invention. Creativity is supported by creative thinking capabilities, motivations, and knowledge. An invention needs to be transformed into a product or a service to be commercialised, to become an innovation. Hence, an innovation implements an invention within an organisation. However we think of an innovation process, it is not always certain that a linear model will be implemented as creativity – invention – innovation. It can also happen that simply creative ideas are shifted into an innovation. In this vein, Schumpeter (1934) distinguishes innovation as incremental or radical innovation. Incremental innovation improves an existing product or service or method or process, whereas a radical innovation makes a disruptive change. For instance, a different version of an iPhone by Apple is considered an incremental innovation because there is an improvement of an existing iPhone, including new technological features and so improving the product performance. The introduction of the internet or augmented reality is recognised as a radical innovation because a disruptive change was implemented, provoking a transformation in the way we live, work, and communicate.

Overall, incremental innovation makes consistent and more secure improvements, relying on supporting existing technologies in line with routines and norms. It is easily implemented and can generate immediate sales and consequently enhance customer loyalty. In contrast, disruptive innovation introduces a completely new product or service or method or process by exploiting disruptive technologies. This innovation provokes new beliefs and it takes more time to be implemented. Although at the beginning, the performance of a radical innovation may not be so good, it can increase a company's profit and bring new value, creating a new market (Table 2.1) (Shapiro & Mandelman, 2021).

Additionally, Schumpeter (1934) identifies innovations in the form of a new process, of creating a new market, of recognising new sources for raw materials, and of introducing new types of business models such as those described below:

• Bringing a new process into an organisational environment tends to occur frequently in the manufacturing industry. For instance, the introduction of bitcoin has been changing the mode of use and transfer of money.

- Creating a new market means exporting an existing product or service into another country or engaging with a different target market. For example, the company Virgin, founded by Richard Branson, started in the music sector and then it developed other businesses in different sectors such as fitness, transport, and airspace, attracting new customers and entering new markets.
- Recognising new products from raw materials considers the process of introducing new inventions through research and development activities and then transforming them into an innovation. For instance, to solve the problem caused by the pandemic event named Covid-19, scientists found a solution that has been transformed into a vaccine.
- Introducing a new type of business model results in a different way of working and so generates new innovation. For instance, the phenomenon of crowdsourcing has been a mode of making new innovation adopting an open innovation approach. The company Lego has been a pioneer in developing a digital platform where customers can propose new potential products to be integrated into the company's portfolio. In this way, the relationship between company and customers gets stronger.

All these innovations are created through creativity. However, to evaluate the level of innovativity and creativity of a business, it is possible to categorise a potential idea as a spaced-out, a blue-sky, or a grounded idea. The spaced-out idea is recognised as something magical. Even though it seems impossible to realise, it may still be considered worthwhile. For instance, imagine that the characters of a novel appear to narrate the novel to a reader; it can be considered as part of our pure imagination.

The blue-sky idea is an innovative idea that has great potential to be transformed into a real product or service to be commercialised. Examples of blue-sky ideas are the first car or airplane.

Grounded ideas show a poor innovation level because they are based on an existing idea that is plain and obvious and can be easily imitated. An example is the opening up of a new bar or restaurant that is not at all innovative but just a business to make money. It can be safer than a blue-sky idea that explores a new market and cannot predict the consequences of a business's performance.

Therefore, when one is thinking of innovative ideas, blue-sky ideas need to emerge. To develop an innovative idea, we would like to propose a model that can start from a spaced-out idea and then move to a blue-sky idea, or from a grounded idea to a blue sky one. For example, we have a magical idea to be shifted it into a blue-sky idea, or we have a mere grounded idea to be converted it into a blue-sky idea (Figure 2.1).

Recognising a blue-sky idea involves the evaluation of such an idea according to the criteria of desirability, feasibility, and viability. Desirability means that the innovation is interesting for customers. Hence, there is a potential demand for such a product; in a nutshell 'customers want it'. Feasibility has to do with the availability of resources useful to develop the blue-sky idea. It is necessary to analyse internal and external resources (tangible and intangible) to understand how it is possible to obtain them. Hence, 'they have got enough resources to develop it'. Finally, viability concerns the costs and revenue of producing and introducing an innovation into the market. It is relevant that production costs are not excessive and it is possible to make money out of it. In other words, 'they have got enough money and have a return of money from it' (Figure 2.2).

The blue-sky idea requires investment in creativity, education, and technology, which are embraced in a cross-disciplinary learning process. Potential innovators should be educated to be able to recognise a potential innovation and evaluate it according to those three criteria. Moreover, according to Hunsaker and Thomas (2017), there is another criterion to be considered, that is, sustainability. In their research, they

Figure 2.1 How to develop a blue-sky idea.
Source: Authors' elaboration.

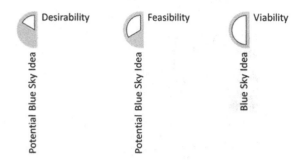

Figure 2.2 How to examine a blue-sky idea.
Source: Authors' Elaboration.

explain this criterion in the context of a decision-making process, but in this chapter, we have included sustainability because it is part of any successful business idea or just a strategy. For instance, for the company Patagonia, the concept of sustainability has been embraced in all its strategies, becoming the driver of a well-run business performance. Patagonia has also released a responsibility programme that aims to offer recycled, renewable, and reusable resources by 2025. With this background, an innovator should question 'whether the business idea is responsible towards community and environment and also inclusive', that can be declined in the concept of ethics, environment, and social responsibilities. Overall, the sum of desirability, feasibility, viability, and sustainability originate a blue-sky idea (Figure 2.3).

Knowledge and Innovation and Artificial Intelligences

As outlined, knowledge and innovation are interconnected and useful for generating blue-sky ideas. In particular, when a company introduces such an idea, it starts creating knowledge that requires market research to validate the 'discovery' that leads the incubation process which converts a simple entrepreneurial intention into something more consistent and achievable. Afterwards, a product is generated and it needs to be tested to be introduced into the market (Bolton & Thompson, 2013). This is the standard and linear process that links knowledge and innovation; however, there are thousands of ideas that never pass into the incubation process stage, or for those that do, an innovator may work on it for weeks, months, or even years before producing the final

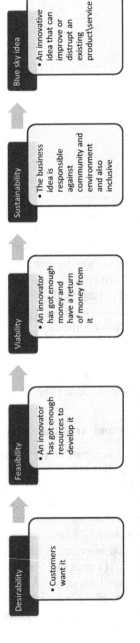

Figure 2.3 The four criteria of a blue-sky idea.

Source: Authors' Elaboration.

product. In this case, knowledge moves from being tacit to explicit which allows companies to get a competitive advantage (López-Nicolás & Meroño-Cerdán, 2011). A greater advantage is obtained by tacit knowledge that is inimitable and unique. It is not codified and developed in a learning-by-doing process. It is held by an individual. Such knowledge needs to be managed and so it involves the process of KM that is explicated in five stages: 1) Creation; 2) Management; 3) Dissemination; 4) Use; and 5) Exploitation (Skyrme, 2012; Fong & Choi, 2009). These stages are relevant to converting tacit knowledge into an explicit type (Nonaka & Takeuchi, 1995) and so disseminated within an organisational setting where knowledge is codified. In fact, explicit knowledge is expressed in codes, symbols, words, and so on that are enveloped in a collective entity. Such an entity can be originated internally or externally to an organisation or through the intertwining of inbound and outbound processes (Scuotto et al., 2017) that evokes the use of KM. In the modern era, KM is supported by technologies that have digitalised such processes (Scutto & Mueller, 2018). In turn, companies are moving in two directions: 1) System orientation and 2) Human orientation. System orientation is characterised by codified (Hansen, 1999), exploited (March, 1991), and conservative (Zack, 1999) knowledge. In this direction, knowledge is pulled out from an individual and reused. It requires a massive investment of technologies that develop web-based knowledge repositories and so preserve such explicit knowledge. It is available in the form of documents and is beneficial for economy of scale, for saving time, and for easy access to that knowledge. However, such knowledge requires high maintenance costs and there is a risk of losing it. In contrast, the human-oriented approach is distinguished by being personalised (Hansen, 1999), explorative (March, 1991), and aggressive (Zack, 1999). Knowledge, in this case derives from socialisation that can occur in physical or online space. Differently from López-Nicolás and Meroño-Cerdán (2011), who found that personalisation employs moderate investment in technology, we declare that even in this case, such investments are high because the tendency of working remotely (e.g. smart working) has allowed for the possibility of being everywhere and having flexible working hours. In working this way, human-oriented people need discussion forums, mentoring, video-conferencing, and so on. Accordingly, it becomes adaptable and manageable even if individuals can be resistant in sharing knowledge and/or challenging an unsuitable culture. The human orientation can be framed within the current human-centred approach that belongs to the context of Society 5.0 (Fukuyama, 2018; Yabanci, 2020). Society 5.0 is a high-smart society where, along with economic and financial goals, it aims to develop sustainability. It expresses the conversion from 'disindividuation' to 'individuation'. In a recent paper, Del Giudice et al. (2021a; b) discussed in-depth this new approach, envisioning the new concept of innovation ventura that relies on the main work of Stiegler (2008; 2011), who considers artificial intelligences (AIs) as tools to empower human skills and to facilitate knowledge creation. Innovation ventura encourages open innovation involving customers and employees (Ahuja & Morris Lampert, 2001). The intertwining of internal and external knowledge is strategically fruitful for a company (Mahr et al., 2014; Scuotto et al., 2017). It is a set of ambidextrous practices that requires a mix of explorative structures and exploitative activities to generate value (Malik et al., 2018). Therefore, companies need to project future trends on which to propose new innovations (Newman et al., 2018) that cannot be limited to the internal and existing knowledge of an organisation but which needs to grasp external insights, facilitated by the use of new technologies (Del Giudice et al., 2021c). In doing so, such technologies support a single and collective learning process and stimulate creativity that is a fundamental pillar of innovation. Yet, a company with a KM capability is more innovative and able to explore and exploit tacit knowledge and get 'the best equilibrium' between tacit and explicit knowledge. Hence, KM employs seven types of processes identified as 1) Externalisation; 2) Communication; 3) Internalisation; 4) Socialisation; 5) Locating & Acquiring External Explicit Knowledge New to the Group; 6) Locating and Acquiring External Tacit Knowledge New to the Group; and 7) Inventing Knowledge New to the Group (Hall & Andriani, 2002) (Table 2.1). Among these, knowledge creation and integration are beneficial for innovation and business performance (Mardani et al., 2018). These seven processes are integrated with three of the four activities outlined by Nonaka and Takeuchi in their Socialization; Externalization; Combination; Internalization (SECI)

Table 2.1 Main characteristics of incremental and radical innovations

Incremental Innovations	Radical Innovations
Consistent and secure improvements	A complete new change
Supporting existing technologies	Exploiting disruptive technologies
Maintaining existing norms and routines	Creative new beliefs
Easily to be implemented	Long time to be implemented
Generating new sales in the short period	Generating new profit in the long period
Enhancing customer loyalty	Attracting new customers

Source: own elaboration.

model (for more information, see the special section of this chapter by Noboru Konno).

Consistently with the digital, modern age, we maintain that AIs are making strong contributions in terms of KM, innovation and business performance. We have put aside the fear of such technologies and so fully embraced the idea that they enforce the sense of 'humanity' of an organisation, freeing it from flat and stable activities and endorsing creativity along with emotions and intentions. In this vein, at the end of this chapter we have proposed a workshop idea to stimulate creativity and innovation among students as well as entrepreneurs and employees.

Workshop: How to come up with a blue-sky idea

The present workshop aims to stimulate the emergence of blue-sky ideas. The participants will be able to practice theoretical discussion of the present chapter and evaluate their learning process through an experiential laboratory.

A mentor/lecturer guides the entire workshop, giving the participants the freedom to develop their creative and critical thinking. Hence, the mentor/lecturer invites the participants to form a group of maximum five people. The first challenge is an icebreaker where participants are invited to reflect upon different ways of using a toothpick (it can be magical, obvious, or innovative; there are no rules for this icebreaker) (time is set for up to five minutes). Then the mentor/lecturer asks all participants to share and evaluate the level of creativity of their ideas. This first stage is used to encourage students to learn how to be creative and get out of their comfort zone.

The workshop then moves to the second challenge, based on coming up with and developing a blue-sky idea. In this section, the mentor/lecturer steers the workshop with some instructions: a brief is handed out and it describes a certain difficult market situation (time is set according to the mentor's/lecturer's judgement).

Through a brainstorming approach, each group starts discussing the problem and comes up with a maximum of three ideas, which leads to the second step when only one idea should be selected as a blue-sky idea. The groups need to explain the motivations for their choice. At least three reasons should be presented (time is set for up to 20 minutes).

The selected idea and its motivations are then discussed with the other groups in order to understand the pros and cons of that idea.

Moving to the next stage, the participants need to evaluate the achievability of their ideas, assessing the level of desirability, feasibility, viability, and sustainability. In this stage, the participants need to state the main reasons for each criterion. Basically, they should discuss how their idea is desirable so that 'customers want it'; how their idea is feasible, so 'they have got enough resources to develop it'; how their idea is viable so 'they have got enough money and will see a return of money from it'; and how their idea is sustainable so 'why that idea can generate value for community'.

In detail, desirability should be analysed describing customers' profiles and needs; feasibility should be examined by individuating tangible and intangible resources needed to develop the blue-sky idea; viability should be evaluated, defining production costs (e.g. variable and fix costs) and revenue streams; and sustainability should be assessed, describing the benefits for a community. Of particular note is feasibility, which should include the use of AIs and explanation of how those technologies can be beneficial for the 'knowledge creation process' (time is set for up to 40 minutes).

Finally, there is the preparation of the pitch stage where each group will present their own blue-sky idea and its achievability (therefore, stages 2 and 3 will be delivered) (time is set for up to 15 minutes) and then the final pitch stage (time is set for up to ten minutes).

In conclusion, the mentor/lecturer invites all the participants to reflect upon their activities through five types of reflections: what happened? (narrate); what did they feel? (emotional); what are their thoughts about the workshop? (perception); what were the new parts undertaken during those stages? (analytical); what was good or bad? (evaluative); and what would they have done differently? (critical) (Neck et al., 2014).

References

Agrifoglio, R. (2015). *Knowledge preservation through community of practice: Theoretical issues and empirical evidence*. London: Springer.

Ahuja, G., & Morris Lampert, C. (2001). Entrepreneurship in the large corporation: A longitudinal study of how established firms create breakthrough inventions. *Strategic Management Journal, 22*(6–7), 521–543.

Ajmal, M., Helo, P., & Kekäle, T. (2010). Critical factors for knowledge management in project business. *Journal of Knowledge Management, 14*(1), 156–168. https://doi.org/10.1108/13673271011015633

Alavi, M., & Leidner, D. E. (2001). Knowledge management and knowledge management systems: Conceptual foundations and research issues. *MIS Quarterly, 25*(1), 107–136.

Andreeva, T., & Kianto, A. (2011). Knowledge processes, knowledge-intensity and innovation: a moderated mediation analysis. *Journal of Knowledge Management, 15*(6), 1016–1034.

Barreto, I. (2010). Dynamic capabilities: A review of past research and an agenda for the future. *Journal of Management, 36*(1), 256–280.

Bolton, B., & Thompson, J. (2013). *Entrepreneurs: Talent, temperament and opportunity*. London: Routledge.

Carneiro, A. (2000). How does knowledge management influence innovation and competitiveness? *Journal of Knowledge Management, 4*(2), 87–98.

Churchman, C. W. (1971). *The design of inquiring systems basic concepts of systems and organization*. Ontario, Canada: Basic Book.

Coase, R. H. (1937). Some notes on monopoly price. *The Review of Economic Studies, 5*(1), 17–31.

Conner, K. R., & Prahalad, C. K. (1996). A resource-based theory of the firm: Knowledge versus opportunism. *Organization Science, 7*(5), 477–501.

Dabić, M., Vlačić, B., Scuotto, V., & Warkentin, M. (2020). Two decades of the Journal of Intellectual Capital: A bibliometric overview and an agenda for future research. *Journal of Intellectual Capital, 22*(3), 458–477.

Darroch, J. (2005). Knowledge management, innovation and firm performance. *Journal of Knowledge Management, 9*(3), 101–115.

Davenport, T. H., & Prusak, L. (1998). *Working knowledge: How organizations manage what they know.* Boston: Harvard Business Press,

Del Giudice, M., Scuotto, V., Ballestra, L. V., & Pironti, M. (2021b). Humanoid robot adoption and labour productivity: A perspective on ambidextrous product innovation routines. *The International Journal of Human Resource Management, 33*(6), 1–27.

Del Giudice, M., Scuotto, V., Orlando, B., & Mustilli, M. (2021a). Toward the human-centered approach: A revised model of individual acceptance of AI. *Human Resource Management Review, 33*(1), 1–10.

Del Giudice, M., Scuotto, V., Papa, A., Tarba, S. Y., Bresciani, S., & Warkentin, M. (2021c). A self-tuning model for smart manufacturing SMEs: Effects on digital innovation. *Journal of Product Innovation Management, 38*(1), 68–89.

Du Plessis, M. (2007). The role of knowledge management in innovation. *Journal of Knowledge Management, 11*(4), 20–29.

Durst, S., & Edvardsson, I. R. (2012). Knowledge management in SMEs: A literature review. *Journal of Knowledge Management, 16*(6), 879–903.

Eisenhardt, K. M., & Martin, J. A. (2000). Dynamic capabilities: What are they? *Strategic Management Journal, 21*(10–11), 1105–1121.

Fong, P. S., & Choi, S. K. (2009). The processes of knowledge management in professional services firms in the construction industry: A critical assessment of both theory and practice. *Journal of Knowledge Management, 13*(2), 110–126.

Fukuyama, M. (2018). Society 5.0: Aiming for a new human-centered society, *Japan Spotlight, 27*, 47–50.

Guerrero, M., Herrera, F., & Urbano, D. (2019). Strategic knowledge management within subsidised entrepreneurial university-industry partnerships. *Management Decision, 57*(12), 3280–3300.

Hall, R., & Andriani, P. (2002). Managing knowledge for innovation. *Long Range Planning, 35*(1), 29–48.

Hamel, G., & Prahalad, C. K. (1990). Strategic intent. *Mckinsey Quarterly, 1*, 36–61.

Hansen, B. E. (1999). Threshold effects in non-dynamic panels: Estimation, testing, and inference. *Journal of Econometrics, 93*(2), 345–368.

Hunsaker, B. T., & Thomas, D. E. (2017). The viability triad: Desirability, feasibility, and sustainability as the new strategic decision imperative. *Journal of Management, 5*(2), 1–4.

López-Nicolás, C., & Meroño-Cerdán, Á. L. (2011). Strategic knowledge management, innovation and performance. *International Journal of Information Management, 31*(6), 502–509.

Mahr, D., Lievens, A., & Blazevic, V. (2014). The value of customer cocreated knowledge during the innovation process. *Journal of Product Innovation Management, 31*(3), 599–615.

Malik, A., Pereira, V., & Budhwar, P. (2018). Value creation and capture through human resource management practices: Gazing through the business model lens. *Organizational Dynamics, 47*(3), 180–188.

Mardani, A., Nikoosokhan, S., Moradi, M., & Doustar, M. (2018). The relationship between knowledge management and innovation performance. *The Journal of High Technology Management Research, 29*(1), 12–26.

McAdam, R., & Reid, R. (2001). SME and large organisation perceptions of knowledge management: comparisons and contrasts. *Journal of Knowledge Management, 5*(3), 231–241. https://doi.org/10.1108/13673270110400870

McQueen, R. (1998). Four views of knowledge and knowledge management. *MCIS 1998 Proceedings*. 204.

Neck, H. M., Greene, P. G., & Brush, C. G. (Eds.). (2014). *Teaching entrepreneurship: A practice-based approach*. Edward Elgar.

Nelson, R. R., & Winter, S. G. (1982). The Schumpeterian tradeoff revisited. *The American Economic Review, 72*(1), 114–132.

Newman, A., Herman, H. M., Schwarz, G., & Nielsen, I. (2018). The effects of employees' creative self-efficacy on innovative behavior: The role of entrepreneurial leadership. *Journal of Business Research, 89*, 1–9.

Nonaka, I. (1994). A dynamic theory of organizational knowledge creation. *Organization Science, 5*(1), 14–37.

Nonaka, I., & Takeuchi, H. (1995). *The knowledge-creating company: How Japanese companies create the dynamics of innovation*. New York: OUP.

Penrose, R. (1959, January). The apparent shape of a relativistically moving sphere. In *Mathematical Proceedings of the Cambridge Philosophical Society* (Vol. 55, No. 1, pp. 137–139). Cambridge: Cambridge University Press.

Prusak, L. (1996). The knowledge advantage. *Planning Review, 24*(2), 6–8.

Schumpeter, J. A. (1934). The theory of economic development. Cambridge, MA: Harvard Economic Studies

Scuotto, V., & Mueller, J. (2018). *ICT adoption for knowledge management: Opportunities for SMEs*. Oxford: RossiSmith.

Scuotto, V., Del Giudice, M., & Obi Omeihe, K. (2017). SMEs and mass collaborative knowledge management: Toward understanding the role of social media networks. *Information Systems Management, 34*(3), 280–290.

Scuotto, V., Del Giudice, M., Bresciani, S., & Meissner, D. (2017). Knowledge-driven preferences in informal inbound open innovation modes. An explorative view on small to medium enterprises. *Journal of Knowledge Management, 21*(3), 640–655.

Scuotto, V., Magni, D., Palladino, R., & Nicotra, M. (2022). Triggering disruptive technology absorptive capacity by CIOs: Explorative research on a micro-foundation lens. *Technological Forecasting and Social Change, 174,* 121234.

Scuotto, V., Nicotra, M., Del Giudice, M., Krueger, N., & Gregori, G. L. (2021). A microfoundational perspective on SMEs' growth in the digital transformation era. *Journal of Business Research, 129,* 382–392.

Shapiro, A. F., & Mandelman, F. S. (2021). Digital adoption, automation, and labor markets in developing countries. *Journal of Development Economics, 151,* 102656.

Shujahat, M., Sousa, M. J., Hussain, S., Nawaz, F., Wang, M., & Umer, M. (2019). Translating the impact of knowledge management processes into knowledge-based innovation: The neglected and mediating role of knowledge-worker productivity. *Journal of Business Research, 94,* 442–450.

Skyrme, D. (2012). *Capitalizing on knowledge.* London: Routledge.

Stewart, G. (1997). Supply-chain operations reference model (SCOR): the first cross-industry framework for integrated supply-chain management. *Logistics Information Management, 10*(2), 62–67. https://doi.org/10.1108/09576059710815716

Stiegler, B. (2008). *Le design de nos existences: à l'époque de l'innovation ascendante.* Mille et une nuits.

Stiegler, B. (2011). The digital as a bearer of another society. *Digital Transformation Review, 1,* 43–50.

Teece, D. J. (2018). Business models and dynamic capabilities. *Long Range Planning, 51*(1), 40–49.

Usai, A., Scuotto, V., Murray, A., Fiano, F., & Dezi, L. (2018). Do entrepreneurial knowledge and innovative attitude overcome 'imperfections' in the innovation process? Insights from SMEs in the UK and Italy. *Journal of Knowledge Management, 22*(8), 1637–1654.

Wiig, K. M. (1997). Knowledge management: An introduction and perspective. *Journal of Knowledge Management, 1*(1), 6–14.

Yabanci, O. (2020). From human resource management to intelligent human resource management: A conceptual perspective. *Human-Intelligent Systems Integration, 1,* 101–109.

Zack, M. H. (1999). Managing codified knowledge. *Sloan management review, 40*(4), 45–58.

Zahra, S. A. (2021). International entrepreneurship in the post Covid world. *Journal of World Business, 56*(1), 101143.

Zahra, S. A., Sapienza, H. J., & Davidsson, P. (2006). Entrepreneurship and dynamic capabilities: A review, model and research agenda. *Journal of Management Studies, 43*(4), 917–955.

SPECIAL SECTION

Knowledge Management for Innovation

'Will Artificial Intelligence and KM Co-evolve for Innovation?'

Noboru Konno[1]

Innovation has become the most important activity of every firm of today. By infiltrating innovation into management systems, it develops organisational capabilities and realises sustainable growth. The foundation of innovation activities is the knowledge creation process. Can knowledge management (KM) become a practical means to support such an 'innovation management system' as knowledge creation? Furthermore, when we think of the relationship between KM and AI, what role could AI play in 'KM for innovation'?

First, this special section of the chapter finds that enhancing the 'dynamic' aspect of KM is crucial for the innovation process. How might KM help new knowledge emerge? We can extend KM into a linguistic system of tacit and explicit dimensions of knowledge. An interesting theory is that the human brain (intelligence) has co-evolved with language, rather than just using it as an instrument. State-of-the-art AI in various forms such as deep learning and semantic language models has considerable potential for KM (Will it be AI or humans who evolve?). Creating Ba *(place-context) where humans can interact with other humans and with AI is essential for sustained KM for innovation.*

1. Management System for Innovation

Innovation is becoming a critical part of corporate management systems (Maier et al., 2015; Rogers et al., 2001). Innovation is not something that happens rarely but rather in everyday practice. Companies must make a sustained effort for this to happen. It is about building the dynamic capabilities of the firm 'in a Schumpeterian world of innovation-based competition' (Teece et al., 1997). Otherwise, they will be swallowed up by the storms of disruptive innovations (Cruz-Sanchez et al., 2020).

Innovation is relentless organisational knowledge creation. It is a process of acquiring knowledge through converting tacit and explicit knowledge, sharing and utilising it, creating new knowledge, and putting it into practice. The Socialization; Externalization; Combination; Internalization (SECI) model is described as the knowledge ecosystem of an organisation with a spiral-upward movement (Konno & Nonaka, 1995; Nonaka & Konno, 1998).

The SECI model has been theorised from the research on new product development, but it evolved into organisational knowledge creation, innovation, and then societal open innovation. The SECI model can be adopted to open innovation among different sectors and the current new societal evolution known as Society 5.0 (Konno & Scillaci, 2021); the vision of a human-centred society that 'balances economic advancement with the resolution of social problems by a system that highly integrates cyberspace and physical space' (Japan Cabinet Office, 2016; Fukuyama, 2018).

The knowledge creation process is 'dynamic'. It is the conversion between knowledge that is difficult to verbalise and knowledge that is verbalised. KM is an effective tool when it functions as a system of knowledge that supports these dynamics.

Our society and economy are fundamentally based on tacit knowledge – just as the universe's dark matter and energy account for 95% of the visible total. Innovation for our future must engage with this latent, unknown tacit knowledge, and the process of discovering and creating knowledge is essential.

The SECI model is also a trial-and-error process at the heart of innovation. It is common to all methodologies and applications for innovation, from design thinking to agile development to lean start-up. For example, ISO56002, International Standard Guidance for the Innovation Management System (IMS, published in 2019), describes the following core operations of innovation work, which corresponds to the non-linear trial-and-error process of knowledge creation: Identify

Table 2.2 SECI model and processes of innovation methods

SECI Model	ISO56002	Agile Scrum	Design Thinking	Lean Start-Up
Socialisation From Tacit to Tacit	Identify Opportunities	Daily Scrum	Observation (getting insights)	Learn
Externalisation From Tacit to Explicit	Create Concepts	Sprint	Ideation	Ideas
Combination From Explicit to Explicit	Validate Concepts, Develop Solutions	Sprint Review	Prototyping	Build-Code
Internalisation From Explicit to Tacit	Deploy Solutions	Demo	Experimentation (story telling)	Measure-Data

Opportunities, Create Concepts, Validate Concepts, Develop Solutions, Deploy Solutions. These can be traced to the SECI model, as shown in the table below (Table 2.2).

2. *'Knowledge Management System' for Innovation*

In this era of innovation, KM is bound to change its form. In retrospect, the KM that is in demand now for innovation is different from the KM of the past. KM has changed since its beginnings. KM for innovation could be one form of that transformation. If we had to describe it, we could say it is of a 'collective knowledge' (Svobodová, 2011). It is not about merely supporting individual intellectual work, but about supporting organisational knowledge creation.

One year ISO 56002 was published (2018), the international standard for knowledge management system, ISO 30401, was already published as a requirement. It is a management system that supports the following activities:

a)   Acquiring new knowledge
b)   Applying current knowledge
c)   Retaining current knowledge
d)   Handling outdated or invalid knowledge

The purpose of ISO30401 is to underpin all businesses so that they evolve the current management system in order to generate value through knowledge. This process is aimed at the usual organisational knowledge, but if the aim of an organisation's KM system is more specifically for innovation, then it would follow the knowledge creation process:

(1)   Acquiring tacit knowledge and discovering insights (socialisation)
(2)   Transforming tacit knowledge into explicit knowledge, and generating collective knowledge through dialogue processes and the like (externalisation)
(3)   Applying the current knowledge base and helping collective synthesis (combination)
(4)   Simulating based on customer and user knowledge (internalisation)

The latter ((1)–(4)) is not for a semantic information database of specific categories of knowledge like the former (a)–d)), but is more like a comprehensive intelligence system in which individuals, teams, and organisations are dynamically involved. It is not just about knowledge that has already been externalised but includes intangible, often tacit knowledge.

Here, we can see much room for AI to support and contribute. *KM World* magazine suggests that KM has entered a new stage (Koenig, 2021). It describes KM development in four stages. It can be seen as a change from a mass of data to a network of knowledge:

> *Stage 1: Information technology – Storing information and knowledge using information technology (IT)*
> *Stage 2: Human aspects and corporate culture – Awareness of the effect of human and cultural aspects*
> *Stage 3: Taxonomy and content management – Interest in meaning, patterns of network*
> *Stage 4: Knowledge graphs – Understanding organisational knowledge as system and semantic network*

The development of KM over the last 30 years has expanded from data and information to context, from semantic content to networks of knowledge. This trend can be interpreted as the development from 'bits' to 'collective knowledge'. Knowledge management forms a core process of innovation management, and this is where the potential of AI can be seen (Figure 2.4).

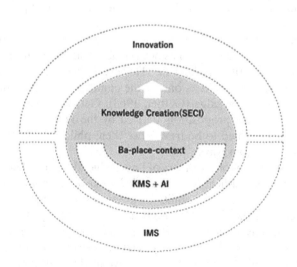

Figure 2.4 KMS for IMS.
Source: Author's elaboration.

Then it suggests the possible impact of rising natural language programming AI, that is, Generative Pretrained Transformer-3 (GPT-3). We can infer that KM will evolve with AI technology. What GPT-3 does is text classification (i.e. sentiment analysis), question answering, text generation, text summarisation, named-entity recognition, and language translation (Mavuduru, 2021) through a human-like interface. It can write codes while giving individuals and teams open and interactive access to share and create knowledge.

3. Creative Dimension of Knowledge and Intelligence

However, one may want to look back at this point. Are the knowledge and intelligence we discuss here the same as the 'knowledge' in current KM and the 'intelligence' in AI? Are we just seeing further development of the current knowledge management function?

AI is a language system, and the present analogy is with the function of the human neocortex. KM has so far been a database of verbalised meanings.

On the other hand, knowledge and intelligence in innovation are 'humane' as it includes intentions, images, senses, and physical elements. For instance, Polanyi's concept of 'tacit knowing' implicates, rather, physical and intuitive or emotional intelligence (Polanyi, 1996, 2009; Sorri, 1994).

What is the nature of knowledge that we consider to be the object of innovation management?

The traditional definition of knowledge since ancient Greece has been 'Justified True Belief (JTB)'. It has been criticised and re-examined in terms of what is to justified to be 'true'. However, when the so-called 'Gettier Problem' was presented as one of the counterexamples to the JTB in the theory of knowledge (Gettier, 1963), Gettier's three-page paper concluded that the 'proposition' derived by the JTB formula is false as it cannot be verified to be true. Since then, philosophers have debated the issue in various ways.

One of the latest findings of the theory of knowledge, aka 'Knowledge-first' does not base its justification of knowledge on the formation of true beliefs. It interprets that the ability to produce knowledge brings justification (Kelp, 2018). Inspired by this insight, we could say that our beliefs are justified only when the dynamic process of knowledge creation takes place. Knowledge is the 'key relations between mind and world' (Williamson, 2000). Knowledge is more valuable in the creation process than in the search for past examples.

Table 2.3 Traditional and dynamic views on knowledge and intelligence

	Knowledge	*Intelligence*
Traditional View	• Justified True Belief (JTB) model • Validated verbalised meaning (explicit)	• Cerebral intelligence
Dynamic View	• Knowledge First (KF) model • Justified belief by act of knowing	• Holistic (whole human, ecological, collective) intelligence

Source: Author's elaboration.

In other words, knowledge is not static; it is dynamic. The KM systems that are now required for innovation are not systems that manage accumulated knowledge but systems that support the management of such dynamic knowledge flow (Table 2.3).

It is important to note that subjectivity plays a significant role in innovation and such a management system. Conventional theories of management, strategy, and organisation have emphasised objectivity over subjectivity. In innovation, however, the starting point is often people's feelings, doubts about the status quo, and sometimes resentment. Therefore, subjectivity directs innovation. Purposes differ from goals (objectives) as they are based on subjective meanings and values.

Now, purpose has become a new jargon for management, but it is not merely a nice slogan. It is a medium that leads to successful innovation projects when orchestrated on diverse levels, through the process called 'purpose engineering' (Konno, 2014). Innovation is an activity that transforms individual subjectivity (tacit knowledge, purposes, passion) into objective knowledge (explicit knowledge, business models) while sharing it as the organisation's purpose.

It is also where KM systems come into their own. It ultimately creates a value that society and people can relate to themselves. It is where an understanding of the inner workings of humanity and society is of great importance. For example, digital transformation (DX) is not about technology but about changing and enriching the inner human experience for the betterment of innovativeness (Stoleterman & Fors, 2004) and using digital capabilities (including AI) to reorganise customer and organisational knowledge to achieve them.

4. Co-evolution of Intelligence of Brain and Intelligence of Ba

The above way of perceiving knowledge is not based on a knowledge model as 'content' in the human brain. Rather, it is the relationship between humans, their emotions and bodies, and their environments. The 'context' of knowledge that exists there plays an important role.

The present author has advocated the importance of the concept of *Ba* (place) in knowledge creation (Nonaka & Konno, 1998). This Japanese word means not only a physical space but also a shared place (whether physical or virtual) for emerging relationships, dynamic context in motion. Knowledge makes sense when one shares the context-place (common to the aforementioned latest definitions of knowledge). This is because intelligence can be thought of as encompassing not only the cerebrum but also the emotions and the body, and we often find that our bodies 'know' things even when we cannot logically and linguistically say them.

Innovation is the process of acquiring society's (lifeworld's) tacit knowledge and transforming it into formal knowledge through a relentless iteration of trial and error. It involves the creating of and experimenting with knowledge such as concepts, models, prototypes, and business models. These processes involve the direct and intuitive acquisition of knowledge through action, and the stage is the *Ba* or place-context. The *Ba* is the basis for empathy and trust, creating intersubjectivity and interaction between the parties involved.

Now, much of AI seems to be based on the neocortex brain model. On the other hand, the *Ba* where knowledge creation takes place is an analogy of the whole human intelligence. Our intelligence is not limited to the individual brain but shared with other brains, physical intelligence, and the environment. (Figure 2.5)

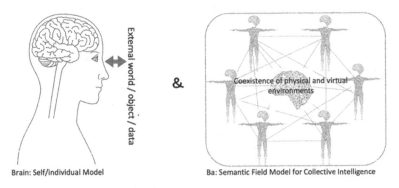

Figure 2.5 Intelligence of brain and intelligence of *Ba*.
Source: Konno (2019).

We can also see this as a shift from traditional cerebral-centrism to human-environment relationalism. It has to do with the philosophy of pragmatism in terms of why deep learning works (Otuska, 2020). Pragmatism is a philosophy of trial and error in the real world. It differs from the traditional search for truth in that it seeks usefulness in a realistic environment. Virtue epistemology, the contemporary study of intellectual virtue and knowledge, maintains two types of knowledge: reflective knowledge and animal knowledge (Soza, 2007). Animal knowledge is knowledge that is like 'a dog finding a bone buried in the backyard' (the dog 'knows' about it). Reflective knowledge is based on beliefs about one's perceptions and is more related to traditional theories of knowledge. Animal knowledge is also associated with tacit knowledge. As animal knowledge, deep learning is a trial-and-error process that learns by connecting data in order to achieve a specific result.

The combination of animal and reflective knowledge lends itself well to exploratory activities such as innovation. The key element that ties the two together is human curiosity (Ohsuga, 2010) as the source of language creation. *Ba* (place) is essential to the premise of such knowledge activities.

What is required is a collaboration between humans and AI. In order to do this, AI must share the same purposes as humans.

An interesting theory is that the human brain has co-evolved with language rather than just using it as a subordinate tool. The collaboration of AI and KM (as language systems) may be the key to sustained innovation. The US neurologist and anthropologist Terence Deacon argued that humans evolved through the mutual 'co-evolution' of brain and language: a co-evolutionary process in which language affected brains (Deacon, 1998). Man is a creature of symbols (symbolic capacities) and communication. For humanity to co-evolve with AI in the future, an expansion of boundaries from brain intelligence to *Ba* (place) intelligence is foreseeable.

5. Prospects at the Moment

Trial-and-error or 'agile' activities in a complex and changing environment have become the new mode for management. It is essential to have an organisational capability that is collective intelligence for sustainable innovation. However, innovation is never a simple process, and an organisational system must support it. This system should have a dynamic knowledge creation process at its core; thus, KM should be developed in a new way.

As mentioned above, knowledge is not data but has value and meaning in a process of dynamic formation. It is good to utilise what we have in our living relationship, and formalised knowledge without context is just knowledge of the past.

Traditionally, we understand tacit knowledge as a physical and emotional aspect, which is perceived as contradictory to IT. If it activates the present and dynamic elements of tacit knowledge, AI will reveal a new relationship. However, AI is a technology, and technology itself does not have a purpose. It is the human that forms purposes; however, AI will most likely be helpful in this process. Toward the future, we should carefully observe the interaction between the two alongside the development.

Note

1 Tama Graduate School of Business, Tama University, Tokyo, Japan

References

Cruz-Sanchez, O. M., Sarmiento-Munoz, M. H., & Dominguez, O. F. C. (2020). Disruptive innovation and dynamic capabilities approach: Sensing, seizing, and transforming. *Eurasian Economic Perspectives, 271*–286.

Deacon, T. (1998). *The symbolic species: The co-evolution of language and the brain.* London: W. W. Norton.

Fukuyama, M. (2018). Society 5.0: Aiming for a new human-centered society. *Japan Spotlight, 27*, 47–50.

Gettier, E. L. (1963). Is justified true belief knowledge? *Analysis, 23*(6), 121–123.

Japan Cabinet Office. (2016). Society 5.0. www8.cao.go.jp/cstp/english/society5_0/index.html

Kelp, C. (2018). Good thinking: A knowledge first virtue epistemology. Routledge Studies in Contemporary Philosophy. New York: Routledge.

Koenig, M. (2021, 5 January). Knowledge management in 2021: KM enters a new stage. *KMWorld.*

Konno, N. (2014). An introduction to 'purpose engineering': An essay on 'practical wisdom' and innovation. *Kindai Management Review, 2*, 52–66.

Konno, N. (2019, 9 December). *Creativity and the human environment: 'Ba(place)' in the knowledge society – knowledge ecology perspective.* [Conference presentation]. Human in the Virtual Environment of an Information-Based Society Conference, Moscow.

Konno, N., & Nonaka, I. (1995). Intellectualizing capability. *Nihon Keizai Shimbun.*

Maier, D., Vadastreanu, A. M., Keppler, T., Eidenmuller, T., & Maier, A. (2015). Innovation as a part of an existing integrated management system. *Procedia Economics and Finance, 26*, 1060–1067.

Mavuduru, A. (2021). What is GPT-3 and why is it so powerful? Towards Data Science, 17 February 17. (https://towardsdatascience.com/what-is-gpt-3-and-why-is-it-so-powerful-21ea1ba59811)

Nonaka, I., & Konno, N. (1998). The concept of Ba building a foundation for knowledge creation. *California Management Review, 40*, 40–54.

Ohsuga, S. (2010). *Language and intelligence – how language was created?* Tokyo: Ohmsha.

Otsuka, J. (2020). *Philosophizing statistics.* Nagoya: Nagoya University Press.

Polanyi, M. (2009 [1966]). *The tacit dimension.* Chicago: University of Chicago Press.

Rogers, E. W., & Christiansen, J. A. (2001). Building the innovative organization: Management systems that encourage innovation. *Industrial and Labor Relations Review, 54*(4), 897.

Sorri, M. (1994). The body has reasons: Tacit knowing in thinking and making. *Journal of Aesthetic Education, 28*(2), 15–26.

Soza, E. (2007). *A virtue epistemology: Apt belief and reflective knowledge.* New York: Clarendon Press.

Stoleterman, W., & Fors, A. C. (2004). Information technology and the good life. In B. Kaplan, D. P. Truex III, D. Wastall, A. T. Wood-Harper, & J. I. DeGross (Eds.), *Information systems research* (pp. 687–692). Dordrecht: Kluwer Academic Publishers.

Svobodová, A., & Koudelková, P. (2011). Collective intelligence and knowledge management as a tool for innovations. *Economics and Management, 16*(99), 942–946.

Teece, D. J., Pisano, G., & Shuen, A. (1997). Dynamic capabilities and strategic management. *Strategic Management Journal, 18*(7), 509–533.

Williamson., T. (2000). *Knowledge and its limits.* Oxford: Oxford University Press.

3 Knowledge Management and AIs for Marketing

'Marketing is the creative use of truth'
(Kotler, 1969) empowered by KM and AI

In 1969, Kotler and Levy defined 'marketing' as a particular function of a business. It encourages buyers in the sale process to improve businesses' performance. Such function leverages on different strategies such as pricing, product development, distribution, and promotion. In turn, a company is customer oriented because it pays attention to customers' needs and changes. Kotler and Levy state that

> Marketing is that function of the organisation that can keep in constant touch with the organisation's consumers, read their needs, develop 'products' that meet these needs and build a program of communications to express the organisation's purposes. Certainly, selling and influencing will be large parts of organisational marketing; but, properly seen, selling follows rather than precedes the organisation's drive to create products to satisfy its consumers.
> (p. 15)

In 1970, Lambin (1970) started talking about strategic marketing, stating that 'The role of strategic marketing is to lead the firm towards attractive economic opportunities, that is, opportunities that are adapted to its resources and know-how and offer a potential for growth and profitability'. Lambin and Chumpitaz (2001) distinguish marketing orientation from operational marketing. Respectively marketing orientation includes a management philosophy (culture), a tool of strategic thinking (analysis), and a commercial activity of the company (action), whereas operational marketing refers the 4Ps (price, promotion, place, and product) (see also Lambin & Schuiling, 2012).

DOI: 10.4324/9781003258056-4

However, in recent times the concept of marketing has been shifting from a traditional view (as Kotler and Levy, 1969; Lambin et al. stated) to a digital perspective. In the digital perspective, namely digital marketing, customers' journey changes; it does not simply rely on the classic four activities of 'awareness; attitude; act; and act again' (Kartajaya et al., 2019) but includes frequent interactions between the offline and the online world. Kotler et al. (2016) describe the introduction of the internet into the marketing arena as Marketing 4.0, which has stimulated companies to be lean and flexible. In this context, consumers assumed the role of being 'prsumers', which means that consumers collaborate with a company to create a new product or a new strategy. Dholakia et al. (2010) discuss how information has been growing in terms of production, manipulation, distribution and consumption that has forged a new class of consumers who have higher expectations and acknowledged experts (Dash et al., 2021). A consumer becomes part of the value generation, co-creating new ways to satisfy needs and wants (Kotler, 2011). It changes the concept of brand image from its static view to a more dynamic lens that is based on 'brand interaction'. Hence, new technologies disrupt marketing function and consequently induce a new organisational environment (Vassileva, 2017). This new environment is characterised by new technologies that are integrated and combined with existing knowledge. In this sense, a company enriches its learning process involving an intertwining knowledge management (KM) approach. In fact, in the marketing context 'knowledge' assumes a key role in achieving a competitive advantage and value. Hence, the concept of Marketing 4.0 needs to combine a KM lens that helps customers' journey flourish from intention to purchase to satisfaction.

AI and KM in the Marketing 4.0 Context

In the interaction between Marketing 4.0 and KM, brand identity, brand image, and brand interaction are empowered.

Brand identity concerns how the brand is perceived by consumers. In a nutshell, what do they know about the brand? And what is the company's projection of the brand? As Aaker (1996) stated, the brand identity describes the brand's opinion and what are its 'promises'. The leverages are primarily intangible and consist in brand identity, brand image, brand integrity, and brand interaction.

Brand identity concerns how a brand is perceived by consumers. It has to do with the positioning of a brand in consumers' mind and knowledge. Brand identity represents a set of characteristics of a brand that a company wants to communicate. These characteristics can be grouped in what a company promises to its consumers. Aaker (1996) discusses brand identity and its characteristics, but he does not consider the evolution of brand identity and its communication by using digital technologies. Nowadays, it is possible to use different tools like artificial intelligences (AIs) to reach out to a wide and diverse group of consumers. Through AI, consumers have a more realistic experience of a brand even though they are not based on a virtual space. In doing so, such customer experience relies on users' recognition which is facilitated by machines.

Companies adopt new technologies along with the classic, traditional tools such as price, promotion, product, and place to develop their own brand identity. According to Rajagopal (2008), brand identity is measured by personality, image, reputation, and trust (PIRT), which was enhanced by Tsaur et al. (2016), who consider other metrics such as quality, awareness, image, personality, and culture. We adapt those metrics in the modern economy including timeliness, transparency, consistency, and monitoring (Figure 3.1).

Brand image relies on consumers' cognitive skills and emotions that are employed to interpret a brand. It communicates quality, values, feelings, and attitude of consumers towards a brand (Paul, 2018; 2019). In a nutshell, a brand image can be defined as 'a subjective mental picture of a brand shared by a group of consumers' (Riezebos & Riezebos, 2003, p. 63) . We also define it as a set of knowledge that reflects consumers' perception. Kotler et al. (2016) encourage companies to address and satisfy 'wants, needs, and desires' of consumers to develop a positive brand image that enhance sales. Like brand identity, brand image is also structured on cognitive and emotional elements. Roberts (2004) and Cho (2011) include mystery, intimacy, and sensuality as elements of cognitive and emotional features. Neupane (2015) affirms that a successful brand needs to be innovative to stimulate always new experiences to consumers. In this line, he adds other features such as being focused, consistent, competitive, leadership, flexible and distinctive. The scope of brand image is aimed at satisfying consumers' needs, wants, and desires, but what happens if consumers become more demanding and placed in a virtual reality? Calling upon Mirbabaie' et al.'s (2021) study, we stress the role of AI as 'facilitators' in empowering users' experience and building up that 'mental picture' of a brand. Including KM, AI strengthens consumers' skills and accompanies it in the process of knowledge creation (e.g. innovation).

Brand integrity concerns the credibility of a brand. As Aaker (1996) declared that brand identity relies on companies' promises; it is relevant that those promises are achieved to keep customers' happy. If a brand is credible, it is possible to enforce trust and commitment with customers. Brand integrity is made of trustworthiness, expertise, and promises (Campelo et al., 2011; Joshi & Garg, 2020). Additionally, other metrics can be considered to measure brand integrity such as clarity, perceived risk, and quality. Reflecting upon those metrics, we have imagined how AI can strengthen and support the development of brand integrity. According to Mills and Carlisi (2020), companies should advance the use of AI in responsible AI. Responsible AI induces business people to keep company promises and be rewarded by consumers through trust and engagement.

For instance, today consumers expect that companies should be sustainable and make a positive impact on society. The social impact is a promise that company should satisfy. In doing so, responsible AI attracts digital talents that are crucial for a company's scope. They also stress the empowerment derived from the use of AI to boost purchase intention as well as employees' abilities. This is the proper context

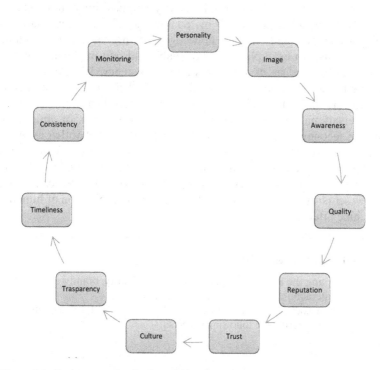

Figure 3.1 Current metrics for brand identity.
Source: Authors' elaboration.

where KM is integrated and exploited. It allows profit maximisation and an increasing innovation rate. As Neupane (2015) affirmed for brand image, it is necessary to be innovative in order to avoid customers becoming annoyed and abandoning them. Such innovation consider knowledge generation needs to be managed to generate a value for a company. Given that the KM process comprises 'acquiring, integrating, sharing and storing knowledge' (Scuotto & Mueller, 2018; Lam, 2000; Walsh & Ungson, 1991), responsible AI is embedded in this process in order to support each step.

Brand interaction is shaped by the active role of consumers, who are also named 'prosumers'. In particular, consumers are knowledge creators of brands through interacting with companies. They experience brand promises and are also co-creators of such promises. Facilitated by AI, consumers have also started to manage knowledge and generate value for a company. AI supports consumers' interactions and stimulates new virtual experiences. Schivinski et al. (2016) sustain that consumers create, consume, and make contributions. Hugh et al. (2022) discuss metrics to evaluate brand integrity, emphasising ethics and sustainability, which is supported by 'conversational AI'. Conversational AI allows inflow and outflow knowledge, allowing for human–machine interactions. For example, a chatbot enables this automatic interaction, reflecting the values of timeliness and consistency. We are in an era where brands continually communicate with their customers and constantly are innovated to be in line with customers' behaviours changes. Conversational AI uses natural language processing or automatic speech recognition in a way humans would respond. Another example is Alexa by Amazon that supports domestic human actions. Knowledge is stored and preserved by these machines, but it is also enhanced by the interactions with customers through 'conversational AI'. In conclusion, a new semantic language is offered through the combination of human–machine interactions.

Workshop: Marketing 4.0

By adopting the KM lens, explain how brand identity, brand image, and brand interaction are evolving in the current age.

Select a specific product category and describe the three aspects of brands considering the following aspects:

Note

1 Transcript of Professor Hawking's speech at the launch of the Leverhulme Centre for the Future of Intelligence, 19 October 2016. www.cam.ac.uk/resea rch/news/the-best-or-worst-thing-to-happen-to-humanity-stephen-hawking-launches-centre-for-the-future-of

References

Aaker, D. (1996). *Building strong brands*. New York: The Free Press. https://doi. org/10.1057/bm.1996.8

Campelo, A., Aitken, R., & Gnoth, J. (2011). Visual rhetoric and ethics in marketing of destinations. *Journal of Travel Research, 50*(1), 3–14.

Dash, G., Kiefer, K., & Paul, J. (2021). Marketing-to-Millennials: Marketing 4.0, customer satisfaction and purchase intention. *Journal of Business Research, 122*, 608–620.

Dholakia, N., Zwick, D., & Denegri-Knott, J. (2010). Technology, consumers, and marketing theory. In M. Saren, B. Stern, & M. Tadajewski (Eds.), *The SAGE handbook of marketing theory* (pp. 494–511). London: SAGE.

Hugh, D. C., Dolan, R., Harrigan, P., & Gray, H. (2022). Influencer marketing effectiveness: the mechanisms that matter. *European Journal of Marketing* (ahead-of-print).

Joshi, R., & Garg, P. (2021). Role of brand experience in shaping brand love. *International Journal of Consumer Studies, 45*(2), 259–272.

Kartajaya, H., Kotler, P., & Hooi, D. H. (2019). "Marketing 4.0: moving from traditional to digital." World Scientific Book Chapters, in: Asian Competitors Marketing for Competitiveness in the Age of Digital Consumers, chapter 4. World Scientific Book Chapters, 99–123.

Kotler, P. (2011). Reinventing marketing to manage the environmental imperative. *Journal of Marketing, 75*(4), 132–135.

Kotler, P., & Levy, S. J. (1969). Broadening the concept of marketing. *Journal of Marketing, 33*(1), 10–15.

Kotler, P., Kartajaya, H., & Setiawan, I. (2016). *Marketing 4.0: Moving from traditional to digital*. Hoboken, NJ: John Wiley & Sons.

Lam, A. (2000). Tacit knowledge, organizational learning and societal institutions: An integrated framework. *Organization Studies, 21*(3), 487–513.

Lambin, J. J. (1970). Optimal allocation of competitive marketing efforts: An empirical study. *Journal of Business, 43*(4), 468–484.

Lambin, J. J., & Schuiling, I. (2012). *Market-driven management: Strategic and operational marketing*. London: Macmillan International Higher Education.

Lambin, J.-J., & Chumpitaz, R. (2001). Market-orientation and corporate performance. Symphonya. *Emerging Issues in Management, 2*, 23–37.

Mills, S., Baltassis, E., Santinelli, M., Carlisi, C., Duranton, S., & Gallego, A. (2020). Six steps to bridge the responsible AI gap. Boston Consulting Group 2020.

Mirbabaie, M., Stieglitz, S., & Frick, N. R. (2021). Artificial intelligence in disease diagnostics: A critical review and classification on the current state of research guiding future direction. *Health and Technology, 11*(4), 693–731.

Neupane, R. (2015). The effects of brand image on customer satisfaction and loyalty intention in retail super market chain UK. *International Journal of Social Sciences and Management, 2*(1), 9–26.

Paul, K. (2018). Whitewashing Britain. In *Whitewashing Britain*. Ithaca, NY: Cornell University Press. https://doi.org/10.7591/9781501729331

Paul, R., & Elder, L. (2019). *The miniature guide to critical thinking concepts and tools*. London: Rowman & Littlefield.

Rajagopal, D. (2008). Interdependence of personality traits and brand identity in measuring brand performance. Available at SSRN: https://ssrn.com/abstract=1309864 or http://dx.doi.org/10.2139/ssrn.1309864

Roberts, R. C. (2004). The Blessings of Gratitude: A Conceptual Analysis. In R. A. Emmons & M. E. McCullough (Eds.), *The Psychology of Gratitude* (pp. 58–78). Oxford University Press. https://doi.org/10.1093/acprof:oso/9780195150100.003.0004

Schivinski, B., Christodoulides, G., & Dabrowski, D. (2016). Measuring consumers' engagement with brand-related social-media content: Development and validation of a scale that identifies levels of social-media engagement with brands. *Journal of Advertising Research, 56*(1), 64–80.

Scuotto, V., & Mueller, J. (2018). ICT adoption for knowledge management: Opportunities for SMEs. Oxford, UK: RossiSmith Academic Publishing. ISBN: 978-0-473-42462-6.

Tsaur, S. H., Yen, C. H., & Yan, Y. T. (2016). Destination brand identity: scale development and validation. *Asia Pacific Journal of Tourism Research, 21*(12), 1310–1323.

Vassileva, B. (2017). Marketing 4.0: How technologies transform marketing organization. *Óbuda University e-Bulletin, 7*(1), 47.

Walsh, J. P., & Ungson, G. R. (2009). Organizational memory. In *Knowledge in organisations* (pp. 177–212). Newton, MA: Routledge.

SPECIAL SECTION

The Role of Artificial Intelligence in Managing and Creating Knowledge in Marketing

Khelladi Insaf[1] and Castellano Sylvaine[2]

1. Perspectives on Marketing and AI

McKinsey's study of more than 400 AI uses cases revealed that marketing is where artificial intelligence (AI) can create the greatest incremental value (Chui et al., 2018). Since the use of digital technologies in business, academic marketing research flourished, investigating topics ranging from understanding consumer sentiment, to analysing customer satisfaction and electronic word-of-mouth-based insights, to improving market performance, to using AI for brand management, to measuring and enhancing customer loyalty and trust, to AI and novel services, to using AI to improve customer relationships, and AI and strategic marketing (Mustak et al., 2021).

Kaplan and Haenlein (2019, p. 17) define AI as 'as a system's ability to correctly interpret external data, to learn from such data, and to use those learnings to achieve specific goals and tasks through flexible adaptation'. AI is rapidly evolving (see Table 3.1). Nowadays, the world is witnessing the application of artificial narrow intelligence (ANI) for image, face, and voice recognition, which enables the development of autonomous objects such as self-driving cars. The future may witness the second generation of AI, namely, artificial general intelligence (AGI), and its ability to plan, reason and solve problems alone. A third generation of AI (i.e. artificial super intelligence, ASI) is also predicted with self-awareness and consciousness capabilities, which is able to perform scientific creativity, demonstrate social skills and express general wisdom, rendering humans jobless (Kaplan & Haenlein, 2019).

AI has greatly impacted marketing strategies including business models, sales processes, customer service options and customers'

Table 3.1 Stages of artificial intelligence (AI)

Artificial Narrow Intelligence (ANI)	Artificial General Intelligence (AGI)	Artificial Super Intelligence (ASI)
Weak, Below Human-Level AI	Strong, Human-Level AI	Conscious/Self-Aware, Above Human-Level AI
• Unable to autonomously solve problems in other areas. • Outperforms/equals humans in the specific area.	• Applies AI to several areas. • Able to autonomously solve problems in other areas. • Outperforms/equals humans in several areas	• Applies AI to any area. • Able to solve problems in other areas instantaneously • Outperforms humans in all areas.
Siri can recognise your voice but cannot perform other tasks like driving a car.	Siri evolves into a humanoid robot with wide capabilities including voice recognition, coffee preparation, and writing skills.	Siri develops superhuman capabilities such as solving complex mathematical problems instantaneously or writing a bestseller in a heart- (or clock) beat.

Source: Adopted from Kaplan & Haenlein (2019).

behaviour (Davenport et al., 2020). Google, Rare Carat, Spotify and Under Armour are among the numerous firms that are adopting AI-based platforms (e.g. Microsoft Cognitive Services, Amazon Lex, Google Assistant, IBM Watson) to increase their customer interactions through marketing channels, enhance their market forecasting and automation, and thus improve their performance (Vlačić et al., 2021).

In the Business to Consumer (B2C) context, AI has already demonstrated great success in many transactions and interactions-oriented industries (e.g. banking, travel, retail, consumer packaged goods). AI solutions are used to process a large volume of customer, transaction and product/service data, generated from internal and external interactions, to provided ATAWAD (i.e. anytime, anywhere, any device) personalised solutions to customers. In the Business to Business (B2B) context, AI is also used to make customised offerings to business customers and enhance efficiency (Grewal et al., 2021). Table 3.2 shows some examples of AI applications.

Table 3.2 AI applications in B2C & B2B marketing contexts

Context	Example	Source
BtC	Banks use business process AI (with the support of IBM Interact) to provide personalised offers for their customers. Such offers allow the banks to charge higher prices to customers with higher valuations, while extracting value from customers with lower valuations. Personalised offers reduce search costs to customers.	Grewal et al. (2021)
	FaceX uses facial recognition to allow retailers to identify loyal customers during their shopping in-store and enhance their service encounters.	
	Conversational AI-powered chatbots help service personnel better address customers' requests 24/7. Through analysing the tones in a real-time manner, service agents can get information on how to improve their interactions with customers, and scripted responses to improve the responses efficiency while allowing agents to handle more cases.	
	Online retailers (e.g. Birchbox) use AI to predict customers' wants, evolving to a shipping-then-shopping business model.	Davenport et al. (2020)
	Fashion-related AI (e.g. Stitch Fix) are used to analyse numeric and non-numeric data to support stylists curating clothing sets for customers.	
	Customer screening AI (e.g. KANETIX) are used to analyse customers' willingness to buy insurance and offer incentives to those with greater intention.	
	Apple's Siri, Amazon's Alexa, Microsoft's Cortana are digital assistants helping customers in checking the weather, browsing on the web, controlling other apps, etc. by analysing speech patterns and providing results matching customers' preferences.	Kumar et al. (2021)
BtB	Companies operating in Alibaba platform use AI capabilities to develop personalised products, learn about their business customers' preferences, track the transactions, identify VIP customers, predict and research customers' needs, and promote personalised contents.	Zhang et al. (2020)
	Firms use computer-mediated AI agents to analyse day-to-day email communications in order to detect critical events and potential crises.	Farrokhi et al. (2020

(continued)

Table 3.2 Cont.

Context	Example	Source
	Retailers use AI-enabled robots to scan their shelves and improve their refilling (e.g. Tally robot used by Giant Eagle stores), and to manage their supply chain (e.g. SAS Viya/ML used by Carrefour to support demand forecasting).	Guha et al. (2021)
	Companies use AI coaches to train salespeople and improve their job skills. Human managers communicating the insights from the AI coaches increases the performance of salespeople, providing the best combination of the interpersonal skills of the former with the hard data skills of the latter.	Luo et al. (2021)

2. AI for Managing Marketing Knowledge

AI is mainly used to acquire customer knowledge through customers' journeys and create relevant content through marketing automation. AI-based predictive models allow to evaluate prospects, their buying intentions, and to identify superior leads (Vlačić et al., 2021). Knowledge-based technologies such as sentic computing (i.e. inferring conceptual and affective information associated with natural language through applying common-sense computing and the psychology of emotions) are also being applied in the marketing area (Poria et al., 2014). Gender profiling of unstructured text data is another AI application allowing the automatic detection of gender in microblogs (Mukherjee Bala, 2017).

Overall, AI plays a great role in creating, codifying, transferring, integrating, and interpreting knowledge, allowing firms to gain a full understanding of their customers' needs and behaviours through their journeys and their numerous platforms, devices, and products (Kumar, et al., 2019). From the customer perspective, AI increases convenience and ease in performing routine tasks, while receiving offerings, communications, and information that are personally relevant to them (Kumar et al., 2021).

Companies need to be market oriented (i.e. able to generate and disseminate marketing intelligence and to respond to it) to ensure their business performance (Kohli & Jaworski, 1990). Marketing knowledge entails processes that generate, disseminate, and store the knowledge (i.e. organised and structure information) related to markets and trends, customers and their preferences, competitors, and the marketing-mix (Tsai & Shih, 2004). Customer knowledge includes the activities of creating, codifying, sharing, and applying knowledge about customers. User knowledge comprises insights related to user experience (i.e. attitudes, values, needs, and wants) and the firm's activities in creating and codifying these insights (Abrell et al., 2016). Market knowledge reflects the external market knowledge about market drivers, stakeholders (e.g. competitors, regulators), and their impact on customer/user behaviours (Kohli & Jaworski, 1990). Marketing knowledge is concerned with managing explicit and tacit knowledge (Zebal et al., 2019). Nevertheless, marketing knowledge is very skills- and culture-specific, greatly complex and, most importantly, highly tac it with lot of non-written outcomes, particularly when it involves social interactions (Simonin, 1999).

3. AI-Enabling Marketing Knowledge Applications

AI applications are usually more suitable for the acquisition of explicit knowledge (Vlačić et al., 2021), and most marketing knowledge impacted by AI is knowledge available in the market (i.e. highly codified and explicit) (Simonin, 1999). Tacit knowledge and its inherent features (i.e. not easy to describe, difficult to formalise and communicate, impossible to codify) significantly challenges AI usage (Fowler, 2000).

Knowledge is 'information combined with experience, context, interpretation and reflection. It is a high-value form of information that is ready to apply to decisions and actions' (Davenport et al., 1998). Marketing knowledge management is concerned with collecting information from within (i.e. owned by employees) and from outside (i.e. available in the market) firms, and thus it should be successful for firms to use transversal marketing knowledge (i.e. knowledge developed internally that is mostly tacit and knowledge learned externally that is mostly explicit) (Scuotto et al., 2021). Table 3.3 presents some AI-enabling marketing knowledge applications.

Kaplan and Haenlein (2019) suggest three groups of AI systems based on types of competencies (See Table 3.4). Analytical AI are what constitutes most of the systems that firms are currently using. Human-inspired AI are systems in which advanced vision tools are used to distinguish emotions. Humanised AI are not used yet by firms, but progress made in developing AI systems being able to experience the human reality are underway (Kaplan & Haenlein, 2019).

AI's high-speed evolution is impacting simple but also complex tasks such as those that characterise knowledge-intensive industries (e.g. financial, law and consulting services), as well as firms' interactions

Table 3.3 AI-enabling marketing knowledge applications

Marketing knowledge	Examples
Customer knowledge	• Using machine learning and predictive algorithms to create comprehensive profiles for current and potential customers, based on structured and unstructured data (e.g. recency, size, frequency and type of past purchases, current web browsing behaviour, psychographic and demographic characteristics, interactions with the firm). Such profiles help improve customer relationship efforts and future customers prospection. • Applying predictive models to engage in prospect scoring, through evaluating the prospects based on their willingness to buy and identifying high-quality leads. • Automating routine tasks such as scheduling meetings, order processing, and answering common questions via chatbots • Using emotion AI to understand customers responses and AI-enabled battlecards to curate firm's competitive intelligence and strengthen its value proposition.
User knowledge	• Analysing large data sets of written and non-written user-generated content (UGC) on social media platforms to collect insights on users' needs, preferences, attitudes and behaviours. • Identifying sentiment, emotions, values and attitudes (i.e. psychographic features) expressed in text, to gain valuable insights for innovation and new products development initiatives. • Detecting themes and patterns in users' posts about their use of products, allowing to collect insights on their user experience and how to improve it. • Identifying how users creatively alter products and services, gained insights for product development and innovation activities.
Market knowledge	• Using natural language processing and machine leaning to analyse large sets of online content published on social media platforms, blogs, and third-party news platforms, in order to detect fake news content that may harm the brand e-reputation and viability. Develop competitive intelligence through identifying keywords or topics from competitors' news releases, social media profiles, and other unstructured data, allowing the firm to get insights on its positioning strategy and for its new product development activities.

Source: Adapted from Paschen et al., 2019.

Table 3.4 Types of AI systems with their related competencies and learning processes

	Analytical AI	Human-Inspired AI	Humanised AI
	• Generate cognitive representation of the world. • Use learning based on past experiences. • Informfuture decisions.	• Understand human emotions (e.g. joy, surprise, anger). • Use the emotions in their decision-making process.	• Able to be self-conscious and self-awarded in their interactions.
Competencies	Cognitive intelligence	Cognitive and emotional intelligence	Cognitive, emotional, and social intelligence
Learning	Supervised • Mapping a given set of inputs to a given set of (labelled) outputs. • E.g. the use large image data sets to separate among the figures).	Unsupervised • Mapping a given set of inputs to a given set of (not labelled) outputs. • The algorithm infers the output. • E.g. speech recognition (like Amazon's Alexa).	Reinforcement • An output is maximised, and a series of decisions are extracted to impact the output. • E.g. Microsoft selects headlines on MSN.com by rewarding the AI with a higher score when more visitors click on a given link.
Marketing examples	Robo-advisers using automation and AI algorithms to manage client portfolios.	Stores identifying unhappy shoppers via facial recognition when existing to activate corrective actions.	Virtual agents managing customer complaints and addressing concerns of unhappy customers in a completely autonomous manner.

Source: Adapted from Kaplan & Haenlein, 2019.

among each other and with their customers (Kaplan & Haenlein, 2019). AI is gradually imitating humans through their abilities to learn and update its knowledge. Nevertheless, the next AI generations need to improve their capabilities to understand insights, intuition, and implicit rules, and be able to learn individuals' personal experiences (Vlačić et al., 2021), and thus obtain the ability to capture tacit knowledge or even to generate their own. As Professor Hawking said in 2016 when launching the Leverhulme Centre for the Future of Intelligence (CFI) in Cambridge: 'The rise of powerful AI will either be the best or the worst thing ever to happen to humanity'.[1]

Notes

1 Léonard de Vinci Pôle Universitaire, Research Center, 92 916 Paris La Défense, France
2 Métis Lab, EM Normandie Business School

References

Abrell, T., Pihlajamaa, M., Kanto, L., Vom Brocke, J., & Uebernickel, F. (2016). The role of users and customers in digital innovation: Insights from B2B manufacturing firms. *Information & Management, 53*(3), 324–335.

Chui, M., Manyika, J., Miremadi, M., Henke, N., Chung, R., Nel, P., & Malhotra, S. (2018). Notes from the AI frontier: Applications and value of deep learning. McKinsey global institute discussion paper. Accessed 20 May 2022. www.mckinsey.com/featured-insights/artificial-intelligence/notes-from-the-aifrontier-applications-and-value-of-deep-learning.

Davenport, T. H., De Long, D. W., & Beers, M. C. (1998). Successful knowledge management projects. *MIT Sloan Management Review, 39*(2), 43.

Davenport, T., Guha, A., Grewal, D., & Bressgott, T. (2020). How artificial intelligence will change the future of marketing. *Journal of the Academy of Marketing Science, 48*(1), 24–42.

Farrokhi, A., Shirazi, F., Hajli, N., & Tajvidi, M. (2020). Using artificial intelligence to detect crisis related to events: Decision making in B2B by artificial intelligence. *Industrial Marketing Management, 91*, 257–273.

Fowler, A. (2000). The role of AI-based technology in support of the knowledge management value activity cycle. *Journal of Strategic Information Systems, 9*(2–3), 107–128.

Grewal, D., Guha, A., Satornino, C. B., & Schweiger, E. B. (2021). Artificial intelligence: The light and the darkness. *Journal of Business Research, 136*, 229–236.

Guha, A., Grewal, D., Kopalle, P. K., Haenlein, M., Schneider, M. J., Jung, H., … & Hawkins, G. (2021). How artificial intelligence will affect the future of retailing. *Journal of Retailing, 97*(1), 28–41.

Kaplan, A., & Haenlein, M. (2019). Siri, Siri, in my hand: Who's the fairest in the land? On the interpretations, illustrations, and implications of artificial intelligence. *Business Horizons, 62*(1), 15–25.

Kohli, A. K., & Jaworski, B. J. (1990). Market orientation: the construct, research propositions, and managerial implications. *Journal of Marketing, 54*(2), 1–18.

Kumar, V., Rajan, B., Venkatesan, R., & Lecinski, J. (2019). Understanding the role of artificial intelligence in personalized engagement marketing. *California Management Review, 61*(4), 135–155.

Kumar, V., Ramachandran, D., & Kumar, B. (2021). Influence of new-age technologies on marketing: A research agenda. *Journal of Business Research, 125*, 864–877.

Luo, X., Qin, M. S., Fang, Z., & Qu, Z. (2021). Artificial intelligence coaches for sales agents: Caveats and solutions. *Journal of Marketing, 85*(2), 14–32.

Mukherjee, S., & Bala, P. K. (2017). Gender classification of microblog text based on authorial style. *Information Systems and e-Business Management, 15*(1), 117–138.

Mustak, M., Salminen, J., Plé, L., & Wirtz, J. (2021). Artificial intelligence in marketing: Topic modeling, scientometric analysis, and research agenda. *Journal of Business Research, 124*, 389–404.

Paschen, J., Kietzmann, J., & Kietzmann, T.C. (2019). Artificial intelligence (AI) and its implications for market knowledge in B2B marketing, *Journal of Business & Industrial Marketing, 34*(7), 1410–1419.

Poria, S., Cambria, E., Winterstein, G., & Huang, G. B. (2014). Sentic patterns: Dependency-based rules for concept-level sentiment analysis. *Knowledge-Based Systems, 69*, 45–63.

Scuotto, V., Nespoli, C., Palladino, R., & Safraou, I. (2021), Building dynamic capabilities for international marketing knowledge management. *International Marketing Review, 39*(3), 586–601. https://doi.org/10.1108/IMR-03-2021-0108

Simonin, B. L. (1999). Transfer of marketing know-how in international strategic alliances: An empirical investigation of the role and antecedents of knowledge ambiguity. *Journal of International Business Studies, 30*(3), 463–490.

Tsai, M. T., & Shih, C. M. (2004). The impact of marketing knowledge among managers on marketing capabilities and business performance. *International Journal of Management, 21*(4), 524–534.

Vlačić, B., Corbo, L., e Silva, S. C., & Dabić, M. (2021). The evolving role of artificial intelligence in marketing: A review and research agenda. *Journal of Business Research, 128*, 187–203.

Zebal, M., Ferdous, A., & Chambers, C. (2019). An integrated model of marketing knowledge–a tacit knowledge perspective. *Journal of Research in Marketing and Entrepreneurship, 21*(1), 2–18.

Zhang, C., Wang, X., Cui, A. P., & Han, S. (2020). Linking big data analytical intelligence to customer relationship management performance. *Industrial Marketing Management, 91*, 483–494.

4 Knowledge Management and AIs for Strategy

> '*Strategy is about setting yourself apart from the competition. It's not a matter of being better at what you do–it's a matter of being different at what you do*'.
>
> Porter, 1987

'Knowing' is predominantly a skill of human beings that also extends to companies as they are the systemic form of the human mind. 'Knowing' is the core activity of knowledge management (KM) that improves artificial intelligence (AI) systems (AlGhanem et al., 2020). As has been observed, knowledge is the main asset of a company where all crucial data are stored in the human brain. Along these lines, companies create their strategies by using their intangible assets, which are less easy to be imitated. Knowledge allows to get a durable competitive advantage even if high-skilled knowledge is limited and costly. It is an essential factor to develop new strategies. According to Chandler (1962), a strategy describes companies' long-run goals, allocating efficiently resources. Again, Chandler defines an entrepreneur who makes strategic decisions as owning the right resources to exploit external opportunities. If we consider the period from the first industrial revolution to the First World War, an entrepreneur was promptly aimed at store resources. With market growth and its increasing level of fluctuation, an entrepreneur moved towards rationalisation of the use of resources in order to allocate the right resources to the right place. This spread the sense of efficiency and efficacy that could be better associated with tangible resources, but what about intangible resources like knowledge? Knowledge includes concepts, data, ideas, and information stored in the human brain (AlGhanem et al., 2020). Allocating knowledge efficiently bootstrapped the emerging need for KM. Currently, the attention of KM has evolved to consider the digital marketplace and to involve new technologies. In

DOI: 10.4324/9781003258056-5

turn, this has stimulated the interests of different actors such as scholars, consultants, managers, entrepreneurs, and so on. According to Ragdsell (2009), practitioners have been implementing a ' "people-centered" KM strategy and then driving it with technology' (p. 4). Drew (1999) analyses how KM can be built into a strategy; Kalseth and Cummings (2001) talk about KM as a business strategy; Meroño-Cerdan et al. (2007) discuss the personalisation of KM strategy; Greiner et al. (2007) debate how a KM strategy can be successful. Going further, such a concept of KM strategy has evolved into the use of new technologies (Scuotto et al., 2018; 2017; Saito et al., 2007). Although the concept of KM has been widely debated there still are some questions to be addressed; for instance, how can KM be applied in our modern day? Businesses are challenging how employ KM into their organisational environment. The scope is to generate a sustainable competitive advantage (Kogut & Zander, 1992) based on: 1) empowering human talents; 2) using knowledge creation and so innovation; 3) employing new best practices; 4) adopting new technologies such as AIs; 5) leveraging economic growth through knowledge. This would involve a knowledge map that asks for a scan of reality. Such a scan can be made by a SWOT (strengths, weaknesses, opportunities, and threats) analysis, a Boston consulting group (BCG) matrix, and the wheel of competitive strategy by Porter (1997).

Revised Management Concepts Aligning with KM and Strategy Development

The SWOT analysis maps internal and external knowledge, identifying the strengths and weaknesses of a company. In this case, the map individuates the 'key' people who can create a competitive advantage. In a nutshell, this analysis selects 'talents' who are main strategic factors of a business. Additionally, this analysis explores new opportunities to be exploited to generate new knowledge with stakeholders. In doing so, this allows the mapping out of the relevant internal and external knowledge (Figure 4.1).

In the BCG matrix, knowledge evolves in line with the business changes in wildcats, rising stars, cash cows, and dogs. The business moves through different stages of its lifecycle as knowledge does the same. We design a new BCG matrix considering 'knowledge growth' rather than market growth and 'knowledge share' rather than market share. A business changes with the evolvement/involvement of a different level of maturity of a knowledge (Figure 4.2). Especially, question marks include high-growth knowledge with low knowledge share. Hence, there is a potential to generate new knowledge; dogs

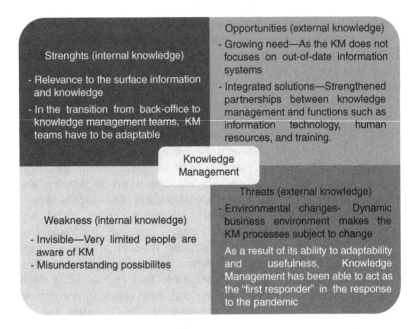

Figure 4.1 SWOT analysis in KM perspective (examples).
Source: Authors' elaboration.

are made of low knowledge growth and market share. Knowledge has achieved a high level of maturity that is hard to change and to evolve; stars are characterised by high knowledge growth and market share. This is the optimum market where there is a possibility of creating new knowledge and of sharing the existing one; cash cows are distinguished by low knowledge growth with high knowledge share. New knowledge cannot be generated but is shared to exploit new opportunity.

The wheel of competitive advantage by Porter (1997) is used to show how a strategy is formulated, taking into account knowledge circulated and shared through all business departments. In turn, a business develops a tacit strategy by using tacit knowledge to achieve goals. Figure 4.3 shows this circular process that involves all business units.

Such circulation provokes two types of strategies, which are codification and personalisation strategy. According to Hansen et al. (1999), a codification strategy adopts a 'people to document' approach which allows to store and re-utilise knowledge. It is reliable and allows to develop a routine scheme within a company. In this case, existing knowledge is used in its explicit form such as databases, workflow, and other

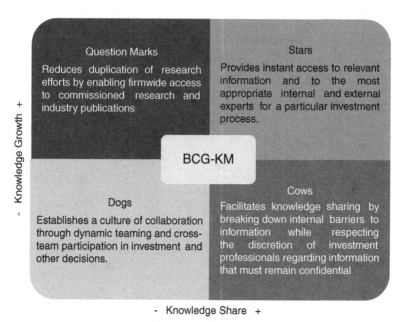

Figure 4.2 BCG matrix and KM (examples).
Source: Authors' elaboration.

business documents (Malhotra, 2004; Greiner et al., 2007). In contrast, a personalisation strategy uses a person-to-person approach that is based on people's interactions. It relies on intellectual capital that differs from people to people, and it is highly volatile. This kind of knowledge is used to stimulate creativity and generate new innovations via the use of new technologies. Technologies help manage, share and create new knowledge. Hence, technologies can support tacit knowledge to create innovation, while they can help explicit knowledge to improve efficiency. Porter (1997) states that a competitive advantage can be achievable via three types of strategies such as cost leadership, differentiation, and focalisation on price or on quality, while we consider adding a codification and a personalisation strategy to be more competitive nowadays.

Interlinking KM, Strategy Development and AI

KM aims to empower knowledge within a company as AI does for the human brain. AI is based on a software programme that simulates the human brain in the process of learning, thinking, innovation and so

Figure 4.3 A wheel of competitive advantage adapted.
Source: Authors' elaboration.

on (AlGhanem et al., 2020). AI implements intelligent human behaviour to codify knowledge and support humans in creating knowledge (Sabri, 2011). AI applies mimic and smart activities that identify the smart machines.

Creating new knowledge via AI becomes easy to preserve and store but less creative. There is still is a question of how AI would replace human thoughts. We do not believe that these smart machines can completely replace huma beings but we support Stiegler's opinion that they can strengthen human skills and competences. AI serves human beings to share knowledge and make it accessible everywhere. Globalisation and digitalisation are the context where the linkage between AI and KM has been enforced. Knowledge is so much less costly, more accessible and standardised if technology is involved. However, AI does not limit a personalisation KM strategy but boosts real-time decisions and stimulates the creative process with people placed at different areas. They create, share and apply knowledge. A KM strategy does not involve only human capital but also new technologies like AI to develop smart activities. Companies thus develop new intangible interactions relying on internal and external know-how. This leads to the idea that KM becomes automated and knowledge is interpreted by machines. As a form of AI, artificial neural networks are closer to the human brain; they work on incomplete data (Alsharhan et al., 2021). AI algorithms transforms tacit knowledge into explicit knowledge and operates with cognitive systems on both operational and strategic levels (Zbuchea et al., 2019). This process requires accessibility, availability and timeliness, and adds more value to the basic integration of information technologies within a company. In fact, when a company starts to include intranets, document management systems, information retrieval engines and groupware, dynamic knowledge where complemented by a web server and a technology infrastructure and less by human skills and abilities. For instance, the intranet allows to store content and share it among all business units; document management systems are used to manage and review repository content; information retrieval engines manage knowledge silos, facilitating knowledge searches and adding new features that can satisfy seekers' needs; and groupware is used to create new collaborations among all business units and new rooms for brainstorming. The latter is highly relevant to transform tacit knowledge into explicit knowledge (Alsharhan et al., 2021; Scuotto et al., 2018). In contrast, AI includes neural networks, robots, and virtual reality (Haenlein & Kaplan, 2019). This technology offers new organisational improvements and opportunities through knowledge acquisition, sharing, and application (Wijaya & Suasih, 2020). In a nutshell, it creates a technological network that allow companies to enhance their performance in real and virtual markets. Additionally, human skills and competences are empowered to be more creative and innovative (Bencsik, 2021). Knowledge is still the key element for a company which is looking for more higher education skills and professionalism. In this sense, a human resource-led approach drives a decision-making process through which knowledge is preserved, disseminated, and stored. This encourages a human learning process of each single employee who collectively generates new knowledge. In turn, a company is a cognitive-based system that is strengthened by AI (AlGhanem et al., 2020). KM and AI become complemetary elements, in which KM shifts tacit knowledge to explicit knowledge and AI offers new mechanisms to enlarge, use, and create new knowledge (Haenlein & Kaplan, 2019). AI seeks to imitate human brains (Avdeenko et al., 2013). According to Bencsik (2021), KM and AI generate a symbiotic flow comprising business strategy, innovation model, CEO decisions and management decisions which surrounds the KM process, as defined by Probst (2006). The KM process is formed by knowledge goals which are set up by AI tools – for example, the SAP digital boardroom – that facilitate the process of decision-making at different levels of a business. Following by knowledge identification that let getting access to the innovation for company, the knowledge storing can be continually updated thoroughly exploration and exploitation activities. Then knowledge acquisition drives people towards the necessary knowledge. Knowledge development exploits neural networks to generate new knowledge (Kuo et al., 2019). Knowledge sharing enables human-machine interactions that can generate new knowledge, which move to the next step, 'knowledge preservation', that 'includes the action of recording, systematisation, storing and refreshing' (Bencsik, 2021, p. 90). It preserves explicit knowledge that allows the finding of a solution to a problem. The user-friendly technology feature simplifies knowledge use by employees (George et al., 2017). Finally, there is measuring knowledge that evaluates companies' performance in this symbiosis of KM and AI. As Singh (et al., 2019) stated, this creates new intangible human capital that is the source of competitive advantage. Such symbiosis becomes the new key element to develop knowledge and let companies be more innovative.

Workshop: KM and Strategy by AI

The present workshop seeks to stimulate new reflection on KM strategies by adopting AI.

In this regard, the reader is invited to map out a business idea, taking into consideration the strategies and relative skills represented in Figure 4.4.

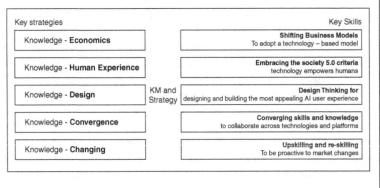

Figure 4.4 Strategies and skills.
Source: Authors' elaboration.

References

Alsharhan, A., Salloum, S. A., & Shaalan, K. (2021). The impact of eLearning as a knowledge management tool in organizational performance. *Advances in Science, Technology and Engineering Systems Journal, 6*(1), 928–936.

AlGhanem, H., Shanaa, M., Salloum, S., & Shaalan, K. (2020). The role of KM in enhancing AI algorithms and systems. *Advances in Science, Technology and Engineering Systems Journal, 5*(4), 388–396.

Avdeenko, T. V., Makarova, E. S., & Klavsuts, I. L. (2013, October). Artificial intelligence support of knowledge transformation in knowledge management systems. In *2016 13th International Scientific-Technical Conference on Actual Problems of Electronics Instrument Engineering (APEIE)* (Vol. 3, pp. 195–201). IEEE.

Bencsik, A. (2021). The sixth generation of knowledge management – the headway of artificial intelligence. *Journal of International Studies, 14*(2), 84–101.

Chandler, A. D. (1962). *Strategy and structure: Chapters in the history of the industrial empire.* Cambridge, MA: MIT.

Drew, S. (1999). Building knowledge management into strategy: Making sense of a new perspective. *Long Range Planning, 32*(1), 130–136.

George, G., Kotha, R., & Zheng, Y. (2008). Entry into insular domains: A longitudinal study of knowledge structuration and innovation in biotechnology firms. *Journal of Management Studies, 45*(8), 1448–1474.

Greiner, M. E., Böhmann, T., & Krcmar, H. (2007). A strategy for knowledge management. *Journal of Knowledge Management, 11*(6), 3–15. https://doi.org/10.1108/13673270710832127

Haenlein, M., & Kaplan, A. (2019). A brief history of artificial intelligence: On the past, present, and future of artificial intelligence. *California Management Review, 61*(4), 5–14.

Hansen, M. T., Nohria, N., & Tierney, T. (1999). What's your strategy for managing knowledge. *The Knowledge Management Yearbook 2000–2001, 77*(2), 106–116.

Heisig, P. (2009). 'Harmonisation of knowledge management – comparing 160 KM frameworks around the globe'. *Journal of Knowledge Management, 13*(4), 4–31. https://doi.org/10.1108/13673270910971798

Kalseth, K., & Cummings, S. (2001). Knowledge management: Development strategy or business strategy?. *Information Development, 17*(3), 163–172.

Kogut, B., & Zander, U. (1992). Knowledge of the firm, combinative capabilities, and the replication of technology. *Organization Science, 3*(3), 383–397.

Kuo, C. I., Wu, C. H., & Lin, B. W. (2019). Gaining from scientific knowledge: the role of knowledge accumulation and knowledge combination. *R&D Management, 49*(2), 252–263.

Malhotra, Y. (2004). Why knowledge management systems fail? Enablers and constraints of knowledge management in human enterprises. In M. E. D. Koenig & and T. K. Srikantaiah (Eds.), *Knowledge management lessons learned: what works and what doesn't* (pp. 87–112). Medford, NJ: Information Today.

Meroño-Cerdan, A. L., Lopez-Nicolas, C., & Sabater-Sánchez, R. (2007). Knowledge management strategy diagnosis from KM instruments use. *Journal of Knowledge Management, 11*(2), 60–72. https://doi.org/10.1108/13673270710738915

Porter, M. E. (1997). Competitive strategy. *Measuring business excellence*, 1(2), 12–17. https://doi.org/10.1108/eb025476

Probst, G. J. (1998). *Practical knowledge management: A model that works.* Cambridge Massachusetts: Prism, 17–30.

Ragsdell, G. (2009). Participatory action research: a winning strategy for KM. *Journal of Knowledge Management, 13*(6), 564–576. https://doi.org/10.1108/13673270910997196

Sabri, H. A. (2011). Making sense of knowledge management (KM), information technology (IT) and artificial intelligence (AI): An integrative approach. *Asian Transactions on Basic and Applied Sciences, 1*(4), 1–16.

Saito, A., Umemoto, K., & Ikeda, M. (2007). A strategy-based ontology of knowledge management technologies. *Journal of Knowledge Management, 11*(1), 97–114. https://doi.org/10.1108/13673270710728268

Scuotto, V., & Mueller, J. (2018). *ICT adoption for knowledge management: Opportunities for SMEs.* Oxford, UK: RossiSmith.

Scuotto, V., Del Giudice, M., & Obi Omeihe, K. (2017). SMEs and mass collaborative knowledge management: Toward understanding the role of social media networks. *Information Systems Management, 34*(3), 280–290.

Singh, S. K., Mittal, S., Sengupta, A., & Pradhan, R. K. (2019). A dual-pathway model of knowledge exchange: linking human and psychosocial capital with prosocial knowledge effectiveness. *Journal of Knowledge Management*, 23(5), 889–914. https://doi.org/10.1108/JKM-08-2018-0504

Wijaya, P. Y., & Suasih, N. N. R. (2020). The effect of knowledge management on competitive advantage and business performance: A study of silver craft SMEs. *Entrepreneurial Business and Economics Review, 8*(4), 105–121.

Zbuchea, A., Vidu, C., & Pinzaru, F. (2019). Is artificial intelligence changing knowledge management? *Strategica*, 445–452. Open access. www.researchgate.net/profile/Stanescu-Dan-Florin/publication/356087095_Psychometric_Consideration_in_Game-Based_Assessment_An_Example_of_Verbal_Reasoning_Game/links/618bb88707be5f31b76281ca/Psychometric-Consideration-in-Game-Based-Assessment-An-Example-of-Verbal-Reasoning-Game.pdf#page=446

SPECIAL SECTION

Importance of Effective Allocation of the Knowledge in AI Context

Vijay Pereira[1]

Artificial intelligence (AI) and knowledge management (KM) are merging (Wei et al., 2006; Shih & Chiang, 2005; Valaei et al., 2017; Lin & Kuo, 2007). This new evolving knowledge landscape will be shaped by AI as it captures, delivers, and accesses knowledge (Wei et al., 2006; Shih & Chiang, 2005). In KM, AI plays an important role by enhancing how knowledge is delivered to people who need it (employees, vendors, customers). Using AI, knowledge distribution and delivery can be scaled up and made more effective (AlGhanem et al., 2020). Technology such as natural language processing (NLP), semantic search engines, and machine learning (ML) are enabling AI-infused KM (AlGhanem et al., 2020). The delivery of knowledge is improved by AI-infused KM in the following ways:

- Connecting the authoritative source and authoritative voice of all knowledge assets to enable the accurate component of knowledge. Some organisations accept this knowledge as a source of truth (Wei et al., 2006; Shih & Chiang, 2005; Valaei et al., 2017; Lin & Kuo, 2007).
- Enabling the personalised component of knowledge to respond to the questions that your users are seeking. An individual receives personalised knowledge that is tailored to meet their specific needs and presented in a way that is consumable to answer their questions. The flow of knowledge throughout the organisation facilitates the development of personalised knowledge (Valaei et al., 2017).

1. The Business Intelligence Concept

Organisations rely on knowledge for building and maintaining their business, since it is one of the most crucial factors for maintaining their market position (Omotayo & Salami, 2018), as well as a valuable intangible resource. The human brain stores all ideas, concepts, data, and technologies. In summary, knowledge can be described as 1) able to be created by personnel, 2) dilatable, 3) can be stored in individuals' brains or any other document storage or computerised storage, 4) can be stored in specific order for easy retrieval when needed, 5) can be shared with others, 6) forgettable and can be lost (Ribière & Walter, 2013). Organisational knowledge management has gained a lot of attention in recent years due to many pieces of research, consultants, and specialists focusing on it in order to overcome the challenges organisations face (Ribière & Walter, 2013). It is crucial to improve knowledge management processes in order to improve AI algorithms and systems. Many studies and reviews have examined AI systems and knowledge management processes. Organisation strategies can be improved through KM, which coordinates between human resources, technological resources, organisational structure, and environment. In addition, KM plays a vital role in educational practices (Ribière & Walter, 2013; Omotayo & Salami, 2018).

Bodrow and Magalashvili (2007) provided the agreed definition of knowledge management as 'creation, communication, and application of knowledge'. Moreover, it is considered a vital tool for improving organisational processes. According to Heisig (2009), KM's primary purpose is 'to improve the systematic handling of knowledge and potential knowledge within the organisation'. In the field of artificial intelligence, a programme can be developed that mimics the human brain in a number of mental processes and procedures, including learning, thinking, perception, natural language processing, innovation, and the solving of complex issues (Ribière & Walter, 2013; Omotayo & Salami, 2018). Using tools like statistical and mathematical methods, AI can be used to build computer understanding and machine learning in the same way that a human thinks and acquires knowledge (Ribière & Walter, 2013; Omotayo & Salami, 2018). In their study of intelligent vehicles, the Authorsassert the utility of feeding back the knowledge generated from the test results of smart vehicles to AI systems so that the AI system can learn more and produce better results (AlGhanem et al., 2020; Almasseri & AlHojailan, 2019; Yousuf & Zainal, 2020).

KM tools are used for knowledge generation, documentation, and sharing, according to Al-Hawamdeh (2002). By implementing AIs to create, organise, and share knowledge, KM tools make managing knowledge easier, thereby improving the operation of organisations (Ribière & Walter, 2013; Omotayo & Salami, 2018). KM tools can be divided into four groups: the first is tools for discovering knowledge and building knowledge structures, concentrating on existing knowledge and current knowledge, and making it available in a structured format and easy to access by linking information, ideas, and experiences. In addition, there are tools for knowledge processing (Omotayo & Salami, 2018), which is the process of filtering, storing, and analysing information. Furthermore, it can be extended to public online forums, wikis, that make the problem-solving environment of the organisation easier

(Bodrow & Magalashvili, 2007). An intranet and the internet, for example, are tools that facilitate knowledge sharing and transfer within an organisation. Lastly, tools are used to analyse and apply knowledge, such as intelligent agents, expert systems, and many others (Bodrow & Magalashvili, 2007; AlGhanem et al., 2020).

Such tools are also used for a knowledge production process, which involves converting explicit and tacit knowledge using methods like internalisation, combination, externalisation, and socialisation (Ziuziańsk et al., 2014). Moreover, knowledge can be created by interviewing experts, exchanging knowledge between individuals, or documenting organisational work procedures (Ziuziańsk et al., 2014). Lastly, knowledge acquisition is the process of acquiring knowledge from outside the organisation and incorporating it into the organisation's knowledge base, such as customer, competitor, or supplier knowledge. A wide range of tools can be used to present AI, including intelligent agents, business intelligence, gadget dashboards, and expert systems (Ziuziańsk et al., 2014; Coombs et al., 2020). A definition of intelligent agents is 'an autonomous system capable of achieving synergistic effects by combining a practical user interface with a system based on Artificial Intelligence, Neural Networks, and fuzzy theory'. A computer system that is intelligent is one that understands its environment and interacts based on data and rules. Intelligent agents can be categorised into different groups: the first is the collaborative or non-collaborative, where each agent starts a sequence of operations after the previous agent finishes his task (Bodrow & Magalashvili, 2007; AlGhanem et al., 2020).

Secondly, profitable economy agents focus on the stock market and online trading by automating deals and decisions. Thirdly, online assistants can learn from user experiences (AlGhanem et al., 2020; Chen, & Storey, 2012). Fourthly, mobile agents are used over the internet, for example, to balance load on specific servers. Business intelligence (BI) was first introduced in the 1990s and has since become widely used mainly in business in order to support decision-making (Watson & Wixom, 2007). It provides a user interface for analysing and drilling down into the data in order to extract useful knowledge and data to help make decisions using a friendly geographical interface, which includes charts, aggregates, and statistics (Bodrow & Magalashvili, 2007; AlGhanem et al., 2020).

2. The Management of Knowledge and the Development of KM Strategies

This process involves the collection, organisation, and share of knowledge, both within and outside the organisation. It is expected that organisations will use KM to accomplish their missions (Wiig, 1997). Organisational performance can be improved by creating, acquiring, and utilising knowledge (Laurie et al., 2005). Knowledge management is a set of organisational arrangements designed to achieve specific organisational goals. According to Drew (1999), KM activities are implemented by companies combining KM with organisational objectives. Companies conduct KM in accordance with their different strategic missions, according to Zack (1999). These findings suggest that KM should be considered a strategic tool (Wei et al., 2006; Altamony & Gharaibeh, 2017), although few scholars have explicitly classified KM strategy. Knowledge is implicit in individuals. There is no systematic and standardised way to formalise it. A personalisation knowledge management strategy is implicit knowledge management (Altamony & Gharaibeh, 2017). Through such a strategy, a company can provide specialised products and services to meet customer needs. Operational knowledge, which is largely implicit, cannot be stored or codified in databases. For employees in such firms to achieve their missions successfully, they must interact extensively with their colleagues (Shih & Chiang, 2005; Valaei et al., 2017; Lin & Kuo, 2007).

3. An Examination of the Concept of Fit from a Contingent Perspective

When organisational characteristics are aligned with their environment, a company performs better (Chandler, 1962; Galbraith et al., 1987). Constant theorists advocate the concept of 'fitness' (Penning & Wilmink, 1987; Donaldson, 2001). An organisation's 'fitness' refers to how demands, objectives, and structures are coordinated between parts (House et al., 2002; Penning & Wilmink, 1987; Donaldson, 2001). The performance of organisations with better coordination is higher (Lumpkin & Dess, 1996). In the absence of alignment between strategy and various related contingent factors, a company's performance will suffer (Donaldson, 2001).

Many contingent theories have classified and analysed competitive environments, corporate strategies, and how they relate to corporate performance. As a result of contingency strategies, successful business strategies must be able to determine how variables under management's control, such as marketing, production, and investment decisions, are related to variables external to management. It is impossible to control environmental variables (Galbraith, 1987). As contingency approaches to strategic analysis have become increasingly popular (Chandler, 1962; Galbraith, 1987), a growing number of typologies in the literature on business strategy, policy, and marketing have described a variety of generic strategies, or strategy archetypes, and the appropriate competitive conditions for implementing each strategy type.

These classifications of strategy types lack empirical support despite some case studies and anecdotal accounts (Wei et al., 2006; Shih & Chiang, 2005). However, any typology's validity would be enhanced if empirical evidence were provided (Wei et al., 2006; Valaei et al., 2017). Based on an objective empirical analysis of strategic behaviuor, a typology is developed assuming that there are only a few observable and recurring configurations (Altamony & Gharaibeh, 2017). It has been proven that strategy variables cannot be considered independent forces, thereby ignoring a fundamental theoretical point; a strategy is a network of interactions among the components that make up business strategies (Altamony & Gharaibeh, 2017). As a result of interrelationships among strategy subcomponents, intra-firm changes in one variable will be accompanied by changes in other variables (Penning & Wilmink, 1987; Donaldson, 2001). KM has been examined in several academic studies (Chen & Choi, 2005; Davenport & Prusak, 1998), but these are too general and fail to address the preliminary factors. It has been very rare to assess the implementation of the success factors, despite their theoretical foundation. Three studies have examined organisational knowledge management (Chong & Choi, 2005).

Furthermore, it is interesting to examine how these success factors are implemented in this industry (Wei et al., 2006; Valaei et al., 2017). KM literature widely regards IT as a catalyst for organisational change (Tsui, 2005). In recent years, deep learning algorithms have improved their ability to simulate human abilities such as 'seeing' (image recognition), 'hearing' (voice recognition), and 'deciding' (analytical processing) (Penning & Wilmink, 1987; Donaldson, 2001). AI tools are increasingly being applied to commercial applications with the availability of data and computational power (Penning & Wilmink, 1987; Donaldson, 2001).

4. Implementing KM: Five Preliminary Success Factors

A KM system is defined by Wiig (1997) as a systematic process of developing, renewing, and applying knowledge within an organisation in order to maximise profits. Besides improving performance, it allows companies to be innovative (Wei et al., 2006; Valaei et al., 2017).

The growing recognition of KM's benefits has led to many studies proposing KM success factors. As Wong (2005) points out, KM must address key activities and practices. It is also necessary to nurture or develop these activities or practices if they already exist. KM should be viewed as an internal environmental factor that firms can control.

Also these success factors were identified by Davenport and Prusak (1998), Ryan and Prybutok (2001), Moffett et al. (2003), and Choy and Suk (2005). Prior to launching a KM programme, organisations need to identify the preliminary success factors. Particularly for newly launched KM initiatives in telecommunications (Choy & Suk, 2005), this is crucial. According to a literature review, little has been done to identify what constitutes the preliminary steps in KM implementation. Knowledge map development, knowledge asset audit, and KM team design are among the five factors. Similarly, Hadlely et al. (2016) recommended business goals, K audits, and K maps.

5. Integrated KM and AI Strategies

When it comes to knowledge work, a knowledge worker creates, evaluates, and applies insights. AI is currently being developed to match the capabilities of our minds (Wei et al., 2006; Valaei et al., 2017). Across the globe, there is discussion about whether such a goal can be pursued and achieved (Penning & Wilmink, 1987; Donaldson, 2001). When dealing with a larger amount of data, it becomes difficult to handle through AI, being the big data analytics to form capabilities (Wu & Hu, 2018; Ciampi et al., 2021; Djenouri et al., 2021). As initiatives has been underway to give machines free will, emotion, and consciousness, AI tools will make a quantum leap. Further, AI provides more training and testing opportunities by combining with a higher level of exposure and capabilities (Djenouri et al., 2021).

Combined with recent hardware developments, deep learning has proliferated. Modern life is increasingly reliant on AI (Djenouri et al., 2021). The financial markets are dominated today by social media bots, autonomous vehicles, and algorithmic trading (Wei et al., 2006; Valaei et al., 2017). Gupta et al. (2013) describe how an *artificial neural network* mimics the brain and nervous system through its architecture. Synapses in the brain change similarly to artificial indicators (Kia et al., 2012). Furthermore, neural networks can be used in diagnostics, business, finance, robotics, mitigation, and computer vision (Djenouri et al., 2021).

There is a belief that *neural networks* provide an advantage over conventional computer applications, such as knowledge-based expert systems, in that they can handle incomplete and abstract data with ease (Sharda, 1994; Kasabov, 1996). Based on similar input data, the system generates decisions similar or superior to an expert, and during recurring learning cycles, input sets and related established outputs are applied to the system (Djenouri et al., 2021). Through the use of optimising routines, links among nodes are gradually modified to increase their weight or intensity, thereby reducing the error between the 'ideal response' and the current neural network response (Djenouri et al., 2021). Due to these reasons, several training data sets are used until the output performance is considered reliable (Djenouri et al., 2021).

6. Contribution of AI-Based Algorithms

AI-based algorithmsuse learning from data and experiments to build a network model and find unrecognised patterns within it, including artificial neural networks (ANNs), recurrent neural networks (RNNs), and convolution neural networks (CNNs), to simulate the human neural system. For predicting and forecasting cretin scenario cases, neural networks, including ANNs, RNNs, and CNNs. have been considered a robust algorithm (Azadeh et al., 2014). For the Customer Relationship Management (CRM) system, ANNs and data mining work in parallel to generate knowledge about customer behaviour and predict their willingness to purchase specific products (Bodrow & Magalashvili, 2007; AlGhanem et al., 2020). Also, the authors emphasise the importance of using KM to feed the AI system in order to improve public safety using the decision tree algorithm. It is essential to feed KM to AI systems, which can enhance AI in call centre domains by helping agents find the best resolution for the caller and customer (Zolfagharian et al., 2018). However, KM should have reliable data sources. It is possible to employ machine learning (ML) by reading the history of customer chat conversations and previously resolved issues with customers to prepare suggested answers to be used by customer service representatives with the capability of customising the prepared answers by machine learning (Zolfagharian et al., 2018).

Based on a study by Tripoliti et al. (2019), many artificial intelligence algorithms were used and implemented in a KM system specifically for the extraction of knowledge in order to predict heart failure in patients. Random forests with a range of between 10 and 100 trees were employed among nine classifiers to get the results (Zolfagharian et al., 2018; AlGhanem et al., 2020). Similarly, within the same medical domain, they use various AI algorithms, one of which is a random forest, which is a collection of parallel decision trees created randomly (Nahar & Ara, 2018). In this algorithm, the output is the average of all decision trees within the forest. Among the studies in the literature, most of the reviews emphasise the direct impact of AI systems and algorithms on KM processes, regardless of the cost or feasibility of implementing them (Zolfagharian et al., 2018). One study found that, despite the positive effect of system output on enhancing performance and data accuracy, the cost of implementing these systems was a significant obstacle to adoption (Zolfagharian et al., 2018). As a result of these facts, we should study the research available in order to highlight this missing point and assist researchers in focusing more on the implementation and adoption of the strategic relationship (Zolfagharian et al., 2018; Arbain & Balakrishnan, 2019; AlGhanem et al., 2020).

Note

1   NEOMA Business School, France.

References

AlGhanem, H., Shanaa, M., Salloum, S., & Shaalan, K. (2020). The role of KM in enhancing AI algorithms and systems. *Advances in Science, Technology and Engineering Systems Journal, 5*(4), 388–396.

Al-Hawamdeh, S. (2002). Knowledge management: Re-thinking information management and facing the challenge of managing tacit knowledge. *Information Research, 8*(1), 8–1.

Almasseri, M., & AlHojailan, M. I. (2019). How flipped learning based on the cognitive theory of multimedia learning affects students' academic achievements. *Journal of Computer Assisted Learning, 35*(6), 769–781.

Altamony, H., & Gharaibeh, A. (2017). The role of academic researcher to Mintzberg's managerial roles. *International Journal of Business Management and Economic Research, 8*(2), 920–925.

Arbain, A. N., & Balakrishnan, B. Y. P. (2019). A comparison of data mining algorithms for liver disease prediction on imbalanced data. *International Journal of Data Science and Advanced Analytics, 1*(1), 1–11.

Azadeh, A., Darivandi Shoushtari, K., Saberi, M., & Teimoury, E. (2014). An integrated artificial neural network and system dynamics approach in support of the viable system model to enhance industrial intelligence: The case of a large broiler industry. *Systems Research and Behavioral Science, 31*(2), 236–257.

Bodrow, W., & Magalashvili, V. (2007). It-based purpose-driven knowledge visualization. In ICSOFT (PL/DPS/KE/MUSE) (pp. 194–197).

Chandler, A. D. (1962). *Strategy and structure: Chapters in the history of the industrial empire.* Cambridge, MA: MIT.

Chen, H., Chiang, R. H., & Storey, V. C. (2012). Business intelligence and analytics: From big data to big impact. *MIS Quarterly, 36*(4), 1165–1188.

Chen, S., & Choi, C. J. (2005). A social exchange perspective on business ethics: An application to knowledge exchange. *Journal of Business Ethics, 62*(1), 1–11.

Choy, C. S., & Suk, C. Y. (2005). Critical factors in the successful implementation of knowledge management. *Journal of Knowledge Management Practice, 6*(1), 234–258.

Ciampi, F., Demi, S., Magrini, A., Marzi, G., & Papa, A. (2021). Exploring the impact of big data analytics capabilities on business model innovation: The mediating role of entrepreneurial orientation. *Journal of Business Research, 123*, 1–13.

Coombs, C., Hislop, D., Taneva, S. K., & Barnard, S. (2020). The strategic impacts of intelligent automation for knowledge and service work: An interdisciplinary review. *Journal of Strategic Information Systems, 29*(4), 101600.

Davenport, T. H., & Prusak, L. (1998). *Working knowledge: How organizations manage what they know.* Boston, MA: Harvard Business Press.

Djenouri, Y., Srivastava, G., Belhadi, A., & Lin, J. C. W. (2021). Intelligent blockchain management for distributed knowledge graphs in IoT 5G environments. *Transactions on Emerging Telecommunications Technologies*, e4332.

Donaldson, L. (2001). *The contingency theory of organizations.* Thousand Oaks: SAGE.

Galbraith, D. C., Soma, M., & White, R. L. (1987). A wide-band efficient inductive transdennal power and data link with coupling insensitive gain. *IEEE Transactions on Biomedical Engineering, 4*, 265–275.

Galbraith, J. R. (1974). Organization design: An information processing view. *Interfaces, 4*(3), 28–36.

Hadley, E. B., Dickinson, D. K., Hirsh-Pasek, K., Golinkoff, R. M., & Nesbitt, K. T. (2016). Examining the acquisition of vocabulary knowledge depth among preschool students. *Reading Research Quarterly, 51*(2), 181–198.

Heisig, P. (2009). Harmonisation of knowledge management – comparing 160 KM frameworks around the globe. *Journal of Knowledge Management, 13*(4), 4–31. https://doi.org/10.1108/13673270910971798

Laurie, N., Andolina, R., & Radcliffe, S. (2005). Ethnodevelopment: social movements, creating experts and professionalising indigenous knowledge in Ecuador. *Antipode, 37*(3), 470–496.

Lin, C. Y., & Kuo, T. H. (2007). The mediate effect of learning and knowledge on organizational performance. *Industrial Management & Data Systems, 107*(7), 1066–1083.

Lumpkin, G. T., & Dess, G. G. (1996). Clarifying the entrepreneurial orientation construct and linking it to performance. *Academy of Management Review, 21*(1), 135–172.

Nahar, N., & Ara, F. (2018). Liver disease prediction by using different decision tree techniques. *International Journal of Data Mining & Knowledge Management Process, 8*(2), 1–9.

Omotayo, F. O., & Salami, M. O. (2018). Use of social media for knowledge sharing among students. *Asian Journal of Information Science Technology, 8*(2), 65– 75.

Penning, L., & Wilmink, J. T. (1987). Rotation of the cervical spine: A CT study in normal subjects. *Spine, 12*(8), 732–738.

Ribière, V., & Walter, C. (2013). 10 years of KM theory and practices. *Knowledge Management Research & Practice, 11*(1), 4–9.

Shih, H. & Chiang, Y. (2005), Strategy alignment between HRM, KM, and corporate development. *International Journal of Manpower, 26*(6), 582–603. https://doi.org/10.1108/01437720510625476

Tripoliti, E. E., Karanasiou, G. S., Kalatzis, F. G., Bechlioulis, A., Goletsis, Y., Naka, K., & Fotiadis, D. I. (2019). HEARTEN KMS – A knowledge management system targeting the management of patients with heart failure. *Journal of Biomedical Informatics, 94*, 103203.

Tsui, J. B. Y. (2005). *Fundamentals of global positioning system receivers: A software approach.* John Wiley & Sons.

Valaei, N., Rezaei, S., & Ismail, W. K. W. (2017). Examining learning strategies, creativity, and innovation at SMEs using fuzzy set qualitative comparative analysis and PLS path modeling. *Journal of Business Research, 70*, 224–233.

Watson, H. J., & Wixom, B. H. (2007). The current state of business intelligence. *Computer, 40*(9), 96–99.

Wei, S., Zhou, Q., & Koval, P. V. (2006). Flowering stage characteristics of cadmium hyperaccumulator Solanum nigrum L. and their significance to phytoremediation. *Science of the Total Environment, 369*(1–3), 441–446.

Wiig, K. M. (1997). Knowledge management: an introduction and perspective. *Journal of Knowledge Management.*

Wong, K. Y. (2005). Critical success factors for implementing knowledge management in small and medium enterprises. *Industrial management & Data systems, 105*(3), 261–279.

Yousuf, H., & Zainal, A. Y. (2020). Quantitative approach in enhancing decision making through big data as an advanced technology. *Advances in Science, Technology and Engineering Systems Journal, 5*(5), 109–116.

Zack, M. H. (1999). Developing a knowledge strategy. *California Management Review, 41*(3), 125–145.

Ziuziański, P., Furmankiewicz, M., & Sołtysik-Piorunkiewicz, A. (2014). E-health artificial intelligence system implementation: Case study of knowledge management dashboard of epidemiological data in Poland. *International Journal of Biology and Biomedical Engineering, 8*(8), 164–171

Zolfagharian, M., Romme, A. G. L., & Walrave, B. (2018). Why, when, and how to combine system dynamics with other methods: Towards an evidence-based framework. *Journal of Simulation, 12*(2), 98–114.

Conclusion

The present book has reached its conclusion. The discussion on know-ledge management (KM) and artificial intelligences (AIs) was enriched by our experts who offered new, interesting insights that can inspire scholars, practitioners, and governments. As discussed here, KM is oper-ating in a new scenario, namely Society 5.0, which embraces the human side of knowledge along with AIs. Different authors have debated the positive and the negative side of AIs, but most of them stress the empowerment that those technologies can bring to humans. In turn, we have moved from Industry 4.0, where the focus was based on tech-nologies, to Society 5.0, which emphasises the central role of humans. Hence, humans are not going to be replaced by AIs but human skills can be empowered by AIs. Along these lines, governments are supporting such advancements. For instance, China aims to become a pioneer in AI technologies, whereas the United States has already introduced new roles that can facilitate individual work, and also Europe is offering a new approach to preserving individual capabilities and rights. The European Commission uses the expression 'enjoying the benefits of AI',[1] aimed at companies that may struggle to include AI in their stra-tegic plan. Again, they stress that 'AI is human-centric and trustworthy'. Strategically, it is opportune to plan how to get a competitive advantage, based on: 1) empowering human talents; 2) engaging in knowledge cre-ation and thus innovation; 3) employing new best practices; 4) adopting new technologies such as AIs; 5) leveraging economic growth by know-ledge (see Chapter 4). In turn, this involves idea generation and innov-ation, which is considered in the form of blue-sky ideas (see Chapter 2) that require creativity and entrepreneurship (inside or outside com-panies) (see Chapter 1). Combining strategy, innovation and creativity in a different order, there is also the sense of communicating and selling the new idea. In this sense, KM and AI for the marketing domain reveal how AIs can generate incremental value. Basically, it is not just human

DOI: 10.4324/9781003258056-6

minds and emotions but it goes beyond that. It is also predicated on self-awareness and consciousness capabilities, the ability to perform scientific creativity, and the use of social skills and general wisdom, which render humans jobless (Kaplan & Haenlein, 2019) (see Chapter 3). The fourth chapter represents the Authors' research identity which have been forged in more than 20 years. The book is insightful and inspirational because there is a need to shed the light on how to intertwine individual life with AIs. It is not just about work but it also includes private daily routine. It is about building the new 'resilient digital decade' (as the European Commission stated). Society becomes an experiential laboratory where new ideas come up and are shifted into innovations. Hence, problems are converted into technological solutions where *the power of human knowledge creation along with AIs encapsulates the essence of modern society 5.0.*

Note

1 For more details, please visit https://digital-strategy.ec.europa.eu/en/policies/european-approach-artificial-intelligence.

Index

Printed in the United States
by Baker & Taylor Publisher Services